AF806443

Understanding Business Strategy

Lourdesamy Iruthayasamy

Understanding Business Strategy

Confusion and Consensus

Springer

Lourdesamy Iruthayasamy
Petaling Jaya, Malaysia

ISBN 978-981-33-6541-4 ISBN 978-981-33-6542-1 (eBook)
https://doi.org/10.1007/978-981-33-6542-1

© The Editor(s) (if applicable) and The Author(s), under exclusive license to Springer Nature Singapore Pte Ltd. 2021
This work is subject to copyright. All rights are solely and exclusively licensed by the Publisher, whether the whole or part of the material is concerned, specifically the rights of translation, reprinting, reuse of illustrations, recitation, broadcasting, reproduction on microfilms or in any other physical way, and transmission or information storage and retrieval, electronic adaptation, computer software, or by similar or dissimilar methodology now known or hereafter developed.
The use of general descriptive names, registered names, trademarks, service marks, etc. in this publication does not imply, even in the absence of a specific statement, that such names are exempt from the relevant protective laws and regulations and therefore free for general use.
The publisher, the authors and the editors are safe to assume that the advice and information in this book are believed to be true and accurate at the date of publication. Neither the publisher nor the authors or the editors give a warranty, expressed or implied, with respect to the material contained herein or for any errors or omissions that may have been made. The publisher remains neutral with regard to jurisdictional claims in published maps and institutional affiliations.

This Springer imprint is published by the registered company Springer Nature Singapore Pte Ltd.
The registered company address is: 152 Beach Road, #21-01/04 Gateway East, Singapore 189721, Singapore

This book is dedicated to my grandchildren—Joshua, Priyanka, Medeina.

I also dedicate this book to my many friends in academia. The teh-tarik sessions, the whatsApp messages, sometimes bordering on sedition, and the discourses during lunch have all contributed in some way or another to this book. The dedication is in recognition of their friendship. Their company has kept my mind inquisitive.

Finally, I also dedicate this book to my many students who have helped sharpen the ideas and concepts presented in the book. Students are the best teachers one can have.

Preface

This book is the result of teaching management and business courses for over 40 years, at the Degree, Master's and Doctoral levels. Most of the ideas, theories, and concepts in the book have been discussed in class at one time or another. They have also been distilled from practice in the workplace. The book draws its inspiration from the works of the major management and strategy gurus.

The book is about business strategy, but not the standard book on strategy or strategic management. The goal of the book is to help the student of strategy and the corporate and public strategist understand what strategy is, the different options to formulate and implement strategy, and the myths surrounding strategy formulation and implementation. The book cuts through the strategy verbiage to get to the kernel of strategy—its meaning, formulation, and implementation. Challenges to understanding strategy are examined, including institutions, public policy, and national culture. Strategy theories are not just explained but assessed in terms of their validity, limitations, and applicability across countries, cultures, and organisations. The thinking and works of major strategists like Ohmae, Mintzberg, Porter, Rumelt, Barney, Prahalad, Hamel, Peng, Kim, Mauborgne, et al. are reviewed and assessed. The confusion and consensus in strategy is highlighted.

The book has several strengths. To the decision-maker in business or government who does not have the time or inclination to sieve through the research literature to update his understanding of strategy, the book can be enlightening. While not prescriptive in terms of telling decision-makers how to formulate strategy (for there is no one best strategy or one best way to formulate strategy), the book does identify broad approaches to strategy formulation and implementation and the underlying principles. To this extent, corporate and government leaders will find the book informative and instructive.

The book deals with strategy issues that are generic and therefore its content is not limited to any particular country or region. The book takes a global and cross-cultural view of strategy, including strategy changes taking place in transition societies. In this context, the book has an international appeal.

The analysis and discussions are presented in six chapters, arranged logically to maintain the flow of the narrative. After the sixth chapter, there is a brief note on "Concluding Thoughts".

Chapter 1 begins the narrative with the opening question: What is Business Strategy? Michael Porter's work is taken as the point of departure. The characteristics of strategy (or tests of strategy) as conceived by Porter are presented. Elements of differing opinions on strategy are introduced. The primary objective of Chap. 1 is to understand the mainstream literature on what strategy is.

Chapter 2 follows from Chap. 1 to dig deeper into the meaning of strategy through the theme "Strategy Making and Implementing". Specifically, it tackles strategic thinking, strategic analysis, and strategic planning. Key works on these concepts are examined, including those of Ohmae, Hamel and Prahalad, Mintzberg, and Rumelt. Chapters 1 and 2 lay the parameters of strategy as we can piece together from the literature. The confusion and consensus in the understanding of strategy becomes more apparent.

Chapters 3–6 take up the four major theories/models in the literature on business strategy. Chapter 3 discusses and evaluates the I/0 model, which is essentially evaluating Porter's competitive strategy. Porter is examined in the context of cross-cultural views and Asian values. Porter's industry analysis is compared to Ohmae's approach to strategy. The significant feature of this chapter is the cross-cultural analysis of strategy, with emphasis on things other than competition. In this way, the limitations of Porter are highlighted.

Chapter 4 takes up the RBV approach to strategy. The differences between the I/0 and the RBV conceptualisations are examined and analysed. The different strains within RBV are also identified. Whether RBV constitutes a theory of strategy is also weighed.

Chapter 5 examines the institutional approach to strategy as the "Third Leg". The role of institutions and national cultures in strategy formulation is discussed, with special reference to developed, developing, and transition societies. The central idea is that strategy cannot be divorced from institutions and cultures. As institutions and cultures change, strategies also need to change. Strategy models that come from the West must be understood in the context of Western institutions and cultures. They may not be relevant to other societies with different institutions and cultures.

Chapter 6, the last chapter, takes up the newest approach to strategy—Blue Ocean Strategy. The tenets of the strategy are presented and examined. Whether blue ocean strategy is "new" or just "fluff" is assessed.

Finally, there is a note on concluding thoughts.

Kuala Lumpur, Malaysia
October 2020

Lourdesamy Iruthayasamy

Acknowledgement

I must thank Nurul Izzati Abdullah for typing the manuscript from my handwritten notes and checking the sources. This was tedious work. She did a splendid job.

I must also thank Nur Sara Syuhada Baharudin for getting the manuscript ready for publication. She did a great job.

Contents

Chapter 1
What Is Business Strategy?

Abstract This chapter begins the narrative to the book with the question: What Is Business Strategy? Michael Porter's work is taken as the point of departure. As the doyen of strategy, Porter represents the mainstream thinking on business strategy. The characteristics of strategy as conceived by Porter are presented as 'tests' of strategy. Five tests of strategy are discussed—creating value, a tailored value chain, trade-offs, continuity, and performance. Any robust strategy is seen as meeting these five tests. Numerous examples are provided that support the tests. Essentially, In this chapter introduces the reader to the fundamentals of business strategy in preparation for a more critical examination of strategy issues in the chapters that follow.

What exactly is business strategy? There is more confusion than consensus in defining and understanding the concept. People like Porter use strategy to describe a business choice and action that is specific, with clear characteristics. Others use the word to mean almost anything that a business does. Sales promotion is strategy. Laying off workers to cut costs is strategy. Introducing new products is strategy. Business expansion is strategy. Acquisition and merger is strategy. Restructuring the company is strategy. Business change and innovation is strategy.

The problem with the latter perspective is that everything becomes strategy. When everything a business does is strategy then nothing is strategy. It does not help provide a meaningful understanding of what strategy really is. We need a more precise definition and description of business strategy if the concept is to have any operational value to managers.

According to Mintzberg, strategy can be a plan, ploy, pattern, position, or perspective.[1] While each definition contributes to a more holistic understanding of strategy and strategy processes, the different perceptions add to the confusion in understanding what strategy is. We need a tighter understanding of the concept and the economic logic behind it. As a point of departure, this chapter discusses Porter's perspective of strategy. Porter is generally accepted as the doyen of strategy. It seems logical to begin with him. But there are other views on strategy, some conflicting with Porter's. They are taken up and discussed in the subsequent chapters of the book.

© The Author(s), under exclusive license to Springer Nature Singapore Pte Ltd. 2021

L. Iruthayasamy, *Understanding Business Strategy*,
https://doi.org/10.1007/978-981-33-6542-1_1

Strategy According to Porter

Michael Porter provides a narrower and a more precise description of business strategy. To Porter, not everything a business does is strategy. In fact, he believes less than 20% of businesses have strategy. Most operate without strategy, including Japanese companies. In his famous 1996 HBR article called "What is Strategy?", Porter declared "Japanese companies rarely have strategies".[2] This upset many of his colleagues in the field who felt how the Japanese could have succeeded if they have no strategy. The confusion arises because Porter uses strategy to mean something rather specific—how companies position themselves to compete in an industry. Attempting to be "better" or the "best" is not strategy, according to Porter. Japanese companies attempt to be the best. To Porter, this is not strategy. Strategy is about being unique. There is no such thing as being the best. All companies can be the "best" within the strategic positions they have chosen. All can be winners. You need not win at the expense of others.

Companies that do not have strategy often do not know they have no strategy, especially if they are making money and growing. A company without strategy may make profit because of fortuitous circumstances. It may enjoy certain monopoly rights or enjoy government protection and subsidies which make it possible for it to perform. But its ability to perform may only be temporary. It is unlikely to be sustainable.

Another reason why companies do not know they have no strategy is confusing strategy with what Porter calls "operational effectiveness" (OE). Corporate managers tend to get obsessed with issues of efficiency, productivity, and cost. They go after the latest management techniques and best practices in the market, such as benchmarking, outsourcing, six sigma, CRM, lean manufacturing, supply chain management, and so forth. There is nothing wrong with this, except that the process ultimately leads to a convergence and not divergence of operational activities. In other words, companies become more alike than different as they push themselves closer to what Porter calls the "productivity frontier".[3] This is a race to the bottom, with low prices, low costs, and low margins. This is not a formula for differentiation and superior profitability. In Porter's words, OE "means performing similar activities better than rivals perform them".[4] In contrast, "strategic positioning means performing different activities from rivals' or performing similar activities in different ways".[5] Porter explains OE and strategic positioning using the productivity frontier curve (Fig. 1.1).

The point is that managers caught in the productivity frontier trap mistakenly believe they have a strategy to compete when, in fact, they don't. Companies operating in this mould cannot sustain competitive advantage because any advantage gained gets quickly eroded through imitation and rapid diffusion of best practices. Productivity gains accrued go to customers, not to enhancing company profitability. This is not to say OE is not relevant or important. OE is necessary, but is not sufficient. As Porter puts it, "Operational effectiveness and strategy are both essential to superior performance".[6] But operational effectiveness is not strategy.

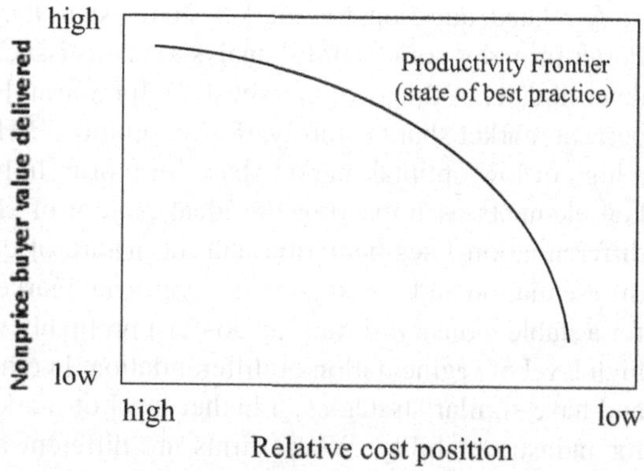

Fig. 1.1 Relative cost position. *Source* [2]

Companies that pursue OE tend also to go for market share in the belief that market dominance will increase company profitability. They follow Jack Welch's strategic instruction to General Electric managers to be either number one or number two in their industry or get out.

The relationship between market share and corporate profitability is not linear. Market share studies based on PIMS data are inconclusive. The firm with the largest market share is not necessarily the most profitable. According to Porter, the "evidence suggests that the relationship between the profitability of larger share and smaller share depends on the industry."[7] In industries where there are substantial economies of scale in operations, larger firms are likely to be more profitable than smaller firms. If economics of scale from production, distribution, and other operations in an industry are not great, smaller firms may do better by occupying niche positions and providing differentiated products and services. In such industries, smaller firms are likely to be more profitable.

This means size and market share by itself cannot be a strategy for better corporate performance. This has important implications for companies choosing to expand through mergers and acquisitions in the belief that size will give them competitive advantage and increased profitability. The strategy question is: Does size matter for the firm? If the answer is no, it is better to look at other strategy options. A higher market share can lead to lower rates of return for a firm.

Porter also notes that economies of scale get exhausted at a relatively small share of industry sales. There is no conclusive evidence to support the proposition that industry leaders are the most profitable or successful. On the contrary, a company can be too big to succeed. Smaller companies often earn higher rates of return as measured by ROIC (return on invested capital). Of course, companies need to have some critical market share to effectively compete. In the words of Margretta, they must be "big enough". This often means about 10% of the market.[8] Companies often assume scale benefits with size and that all must move down the scale curve to reduce unit cost of production. In reality, most industries have multiple scale curves, which means companies can compete differently in the industry.

A related question for market share is: Is there an optimum size for a firm? Porter provides some helpful analysis on this issue. He explains that there are many determinants of the ideal market share for a firm. He points out "that holding a 100 percent market share is rarely, if ever, optimal."[9] He then lists the factors favouring a high or low optimal market share for a firm. In his analysis, Porter identifies two key elements as impacting the ideal pattern of shares in an industry—degree of differentiation / segmentation and the nature of competitors. Where there is little differentiation and few segments, significant market share differences are necessary for a stable industry. Firms can co-exist profitably with similar shares where there is high level of segmentation or differentiation. In other words, where firms are similar and have similar strategies, a higher level of market share differential is necessary for industry stability. Where firms are different and follow different competitive strategies, they can co-exist with lower market share differentials. Clearly, industry structure is an important determinant of the importance of market share for a firm.

Porter also points out the relevance of the nature of competitors to market share. He says: "Where competitors are bad competitors, large share differences among firms are necessary to preserve stability…"[10] (stability of industry) and "where competitors are good competitors, conversely, little share differential may be necessary…".[11]

Porter has good advice for firms that aggressively pursue market share as a strategy. They must be careful not to drive competitors to desperation, if they want to maintain stability in the industry. Too much success against competitors can drive good competitors into bad ones. Porter stresses: "Beyond a point, growing invites problems that are best avoided by ceding share to good competitors."[12] A better course of action for a market leader is to look for growth elsewhere rather than to seek for more share in the same industry. The firm could also find ways to increase the overall industry size or profitability, thereby expanding the opportunity pie for everyone and still maintaining industry stability.

Porter's Characteristics of Strategy

In the Porter perspective, business strategy is defined in terms of certain characteristics. The elements discussed below comprise the principal characteristics of strategy. They constitute the "tests" of any good and robust strategy.[13]

Test 1: Creating Value

The fundamental test of any strategy is that it must create value for customers. To create value, the strategy must present a unique value proposition that is not only different from competitors but also sustainable. This is the first test of strategy. Strategy is not about being "better" than your competitor or becoming the "best" company. It is being different from the rest of the pack, offering something that is unique and of value to the customer. The important point is that what the company offers must be of value to the customer, or at least perceived to be valuable by the customer.

Here the marketing concepts of value and quality are relevant to strategy. It is not the strategist who determines what is value and quality. Value and quality are determined by the customer. Strategy is about meeting the value and quality needs of the customer. The value proposition of the business is directed to meeting the needs of the customer. Value flows up from the customer, not down from the strategist. Strategy is about being customer driven. This has implications for the organisation, its management, and operations. The entire business organisation and its operations must be designed to support the value creation proposition of its strategy. This is the concept of "fit" between strategy and operations discussed later under value chain.

Because business operation is concerned with creating value for customers, which is what marketing is all about, does it follow that strategy is marketing? There is clearly an overlap between business strategy and marketing theory. Marketing is about satisfying customer needs for products and services in a cost-effective manner. This involves developing marketing strategies around product, price, distribution, and promotion. Two fundamental concepts in marketing are customer and competitor analysis. Drucker best described the nexus between business and marketing when he said the purpose of business is to create a customer. He further stressed the link between business and marketing when he posited that business has only two functions—marketing and innovation.[14] Both these functions involve satisfying customer needs.

Does this mean business strategy is marketing? While there is a close nexus between the two and both disciplines are built around the customer and his needs, business strategy is not marketing. It goes beyond market segmentation and customer and competitor analysis. The primary focus of business strategy is industry analysis and dynamics, strategy choices, and building the value chain activities required to support and sustain the strategy choices made by the company. Strategy is more than marketing.

To offer a unique value proposition to customers, a company needs to choose the kind of value it wants to offer. In selecting to offer a unique set of values, the company deliberately decides to forgo offering other values. A trade-off is needed between what values the company wants to offer. It cannot offer all values or offer the same values as its competitors. If it offers the same values to customers as its rivals, it will not have a sustainable strategy. There will be no competitive advantage, only competitive parity. To have competitive advantage, the company must position itself in the industry as a unique player, offering a unique set of values to carefully selected customers, with a tailor-made value chain to support its value offerings. To Porter, this is strategy. He defines strategy as the "creation of a unique and valuable position, involving a different set of activities."[15] There can only be a unique value proposition if there is a unique set of supporting activities. A company's value chain is intimately linked to its capacity to offer unique value to customers. Different value offerings require different supporting value chain activities. In Porter's strategy, there is a close link between positioning, values, and operations.

To understand the value proposition of a company, there is a need to understand its composition. A value proposition is built around three elements:

- Customer
- Customer Needs
- Relative Price and Cost.

These constitute the three legs of a value proposition triangle. The initial value concepts were developed by Porter in his 1996 HBR article "What is Strategy?" in which he described three bases of positioning—variety (product based), needs (customer segment), and access (customer accessibility). Since then, these concepts have been refined.

Customer

A key question for strategy is: What customers do we want to serve and what customers we don't want to serve? With some exceptions, it is not possible for a company to serve all customers well because the needs of customers vary. To meet customer needs better than its competitors, a company needs to develop a unique set of operations and activities to support its value proposition.

A company cannot serve different customers with the same value chain activities. To serve different customers, a company needs to develop different sets of support activities. For most companies, this is difficult not only because of resource and competency limitations but, more importantly, because of incompatibility between different sets of value chain activities in the company. For a value chain to provide support to strategy, there must be internal consistency and "fit" among the numerous activities that a company performs. If a company chooses to serve different customer segments with different needs, it will be hard to achieve the needed fit and compatibility in the activities to be performed.

This underscores the importance of market segmentation and selecting the target customers to serve. There is a need for trade-offs. The company needs to focus. If it chooses to serve one group of customers, it cannot serve other groups of customers at the same time. To serve other customers, the company needs a different organisation, a different strategy, and a different set of support activities.

One way a strategy can create value for customers is by focusing on definite customer segments and customer needs. Porter quotes several examples in his 1996 HBR article. Southwest Airlines focus on price-sensitive customers who want to fly but cannot afford full-services airline. IKEA serves customers who are prepared to trade-off service for cost. Walmart started with customers in small, rural towns and avoided the big cities. Jiffy Lube International, a lubricant supplier, focuses on customers who want a quick oil change for their automobiles. All these companies developed strategies focused on specific customers and their needs. Customer focus represents standard market segmentation.

Customer Needs

Focusing on customer is focusing on customer needs. The idea is to identify what customers need and satisfy the needs better than your rivals. Walmart, IKEA, Jiffy Lube, and Southwest Airlines all target the special needs of a sub-set of customers. Here the company chooses the need it will serve. Its strategy is based on serving that need better than its competitors. Magretta provides several examples of companies that have built their strategies on specific need of customers.[16]

Enterprise Rent-A-Car competes against Hertz and Avis with a strategy that is distinct and different. Its strategy is based on serving a different need of customers for car rentals. Hertz and Avis built their strategy on business travellers looking to rent cars when they are away from home travelling. Enterprise focuses on people who need to rent cars for periods of time when their own vehicles are not available for whatever reasons. Enterprise chose to serve a different need, supported by a different set of value activities. Enterprise is not the best car rental company, but it meets a unique need. It presents a valuable proposition to customers that is different from competitors.

Similarly, Zipcar chooses to follow a different path. It targets different customer needs. It focuses on customers who do not own a car but occasionally need a car for short periods of time. It specialises in this niche market.

Businesses exist to serve customers, more specifically, the needs of customers. This means, the starting point for a business is finding out what are the current needs of customers and then deciding how best it can meet those needs better than competitors can. You cannot meet those needs by doing what your rivals are doing. It is not enough to be better than your competitors. You need to be different. In the words of Magretta, "The first test of a strategy is whether your value proposition is different from your rivals."[17] If not, you don't have a strategy by Porter's definition.

This is what positioning is about. Industry analysis should lead a company to develop positioning maps that identify the relative positions of its competitors in the industry. Rivals will all occupy certain positions in the industry and serve certain customers and needs. To compete, a business has to identify gaps in the market through market segmentation and then decide which gap it wants to fill. In other words, the business targets the market it wants to serve. The selection of customers and needs to serve depends on market structures, competition in the market, and the resources and competencies of the company. Based on this, the company selects a position in the market—where and how to compete. This then becomes the company strategy, built on a unique value proposition and supported by a unique value chain. Companies with clear strategies have unique ways to compete. Southwest Airlines, AirAsia, Walmart, IKEA, Apple, Google, and Facebook all have clear strategies to compete in the market.

Relative Price and Cost

The third leg of value proposition is relative price and cost. The objective of strategy is to create a competitive advantage for the business. Competitive advantage is created when a company offers a unique value to customers in a distinctive way. Competitive advantage is a relative concept. It is always relative to your competitors. How does your strategy help you to perform better than your rivals? That is the key question. Implicit in that question is, how do you measure performance? Business is about performance and therefore strategy must be linked to the financial performance and P&L of the company. In assessing strategy and competitive advantage, financial returns must be measured relative to other companies in the industry. There is need to compare with rivals and the industry. How the company is performing relative to its competitors and the industry is the key test. This is usually captured using returns on invested capital (ROIC).

To understand competitive advantage, we need to understand the relationship between relative price and relative cost. A company has competitive advantage if it can operate at higher relative price or lower relative cost or both. If a company is less profitable than its competitors, it means it is operating with lower relative prices or higher relative costs or both. Relative price and cost are the two components of superior profitability.

A company can command higher or premium price only if it offers products or services that are unique and valuable to customers. Premium pricing is related to superior value and superior value comes from differentiation. The goal of strategy is superior profitability. One source of superior profitability is higher prices achieved through differentiation.

The second source of superior profitability is lower cost than your rivals. The company reduces relative cost by being more efficient and productive in all its operations and activities. Its value chain is more efficient. The cost advantage may come from lower operating costs or using capital more efficiently. These companies are more than "low-cost producers." The cost advantage comes from performing all the activities of the value chain at the lowest possible cost. It involves management, organisation, and operations—such as restructuring, re-engineering, and best practices. Companies like Dell, Walmart, IKEA, Nucor, and Southwest have perfected cost management across their entire operations.

The relative price-cost analysis is significant for strategy because it explains what Porter means by differentiation and how to achieve differentiation. Value propositions are created through relative price-cost differences between rivals and those differences explain differences in profitability between companies operating in the same industry. The goal of strategy is to shift relative price or relative cost in order to achieve competitive advantage for the company.

Test 2: Tailored Value Chain

Porter's second test of strategy is a tailored value chain. Porter introduced the concept of value chain in his 1985 book **Competitive Advantage**. He refined the concept in his 1996 HBR article "What is Strategy?".

To Porter, the value chain of a company is crucial to competitive strategy. It is the value chain that enables a company to differentiate itself from its rivals. More importantly, it is the value chain that enables a company to sustain its competitive advantage. A value proposition is not sustainable without a supporting, tailored value chain. Many strategists believe competitive advantage is not sustainable because of imitation by rivals. A successful strategy will be quickly copied by competitors. Best practices get diffused throughout the industry through imitation. Benchmarking compounds the problem as companies move toward some industry standardisation. Outsourcing, often to the same company, adds to the standardisation process. Outsourcing does not support differentiation. The end result is, all companies competing in an industry become more and more alike, with similar strategies and value offerings. The industry then begins to suffer from hyper-competition where competition is reduced to price. This becomes a race to the bottom. Many industries in Japan have experienced this phenomenon. There is little differentiation. Companies survive with small margins.

Porter believes this form of competition is not inevitable in an industry. In fact, he thinks it is self-inflicted. It is self-inflicted because the companies competing have failed to develop their own unique, tailored value chain activities to support their value proposition. A value proposition, however unique, is not sustainable without a value chain tailor-built to support the company's value aspirations. Strategies built on value or cost can be copied by rivals, but the value chain activities of a company are more difficult to copy or replicate. This is provided the value chain consists of activities that are internally consistent and are embedded in the organisation, management and operating systems of the company. If the value chain is a "system" of activities that supports the strategy of a company, it is difficult for rivals to copy and replicate the activities as a functioning system in their own organisations. Rivals may copy some specific activity or practice, but they cannot successfully copy and implement a whole value chain system of another company. This is because a value chain of a company, if specific and tailor-made, is embedded in the corporate culture and values of the company. It cannot just be plucked and transplanted in another company, with a different history, culture, values, and operating system. This explains why attempts to copy Toyota's operating system and lean manufacturing by rivals have not met with much success. Rivals find it difficult to copy Toyota because its value chain is not disparate but functions as a system of reinforcing activities.

This explains why Porter places so much emphasis on developing a tailored value chain to support strategy. Without it, either the strategy will fail because of poor operational support or the strategy will not provide any sustainable competitive advantage.

What are the tests of a good value chain? Porter identifies several characteristics of an effective value chain. He begins by differentiating "activities" from "functions".

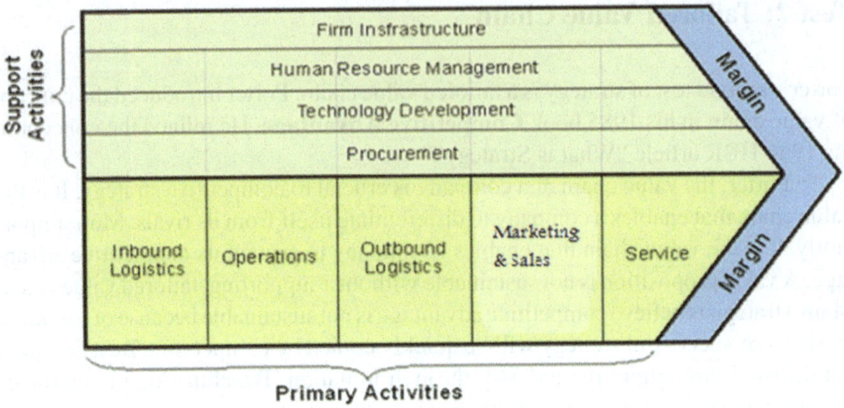

Fig. 1.2 The Generic Value Chain. *Source* [8]

Managers tend to talk in terms of functions, such as manufacturing, marketing, HRM, logistics, and so on. Porter feels functions are too broad and general to be operationally useful to strategy. He breaks down functions into specific activities that a company must perform to support its strategy.

In his book **Competitive Advantage**, Porter identifies nine categories of activities under two labels—primary and supportive.[18] The activities cover the whole gambit of management operations, from inbound logistics to providing service to customers after sales. The support activities include all those activities that provide support to the primary activities of the firm. Porter calls them firm infrastructure, HRM, technology development, and procurement (Fig. 1.2).

In Porter's model, the operations a company performs are analysed in terms of specific activities and their relationship to the company strategy. Every activity is seen as adding or subtracting value for the customer. The set of activities performed must contribute to the value proposition of the company in terms of higher prices or lower costs. In other words, the value chain activities must help the company gain competitive advantage, either through differentiation or lower costs.

By being specific and tying operational activities to company strategy, Porter provides a methodology for assessing and evaluating the operational activities of a firm. The methodology has general applicability. It applies to operational units in business, government, and nonprofits. The mission and strategy of the operating units may be different in different environments, but the relationship between their strategy and their value chain activities remains the same. The activities they perform everyday must support the strategy they have chosen. There cannot be incongruence between value chain activities and strategy. This is the first test of a strong value chain.

A company that competes on lower cost, such as Southwest, AirAsia, Walmart or IKEA, needs to develop a tailored set of activities to support its cost strategy. The host of activities that Southwest performs and the decisions it makes are all geared to reducing cost of operations. From the aircraft it uses, selection of airports and routes, turn-around time, no meals, no seat assignments, no interline baggage transfers to HR and union management are all targeted to reduce cost and increase productivity. Southwest's mastery of cost management along all its value chain activities is what explains the success and sustainability of its cost strategy. Similarly, IKEA is able to succeed in the tough furniture retailing industry because it has successfully developed a unique set of activities to reduce cost of operations and offer value to its customers. On the other hand, Apple which competes on differentiation and premium pricing has its own set of activities that contributes to offering higher customer value. These activities extend from product leadership and innovation to distribution, sales, and brand management. The value chain activities performed by Southwest and Apple are directed to achieving different goals. In the case of Southwest, it is cost reduction. In the case of Apple, it is differentiation.

A second test of an effective value chain is what Porter calls "strategic fit". He identified three types of fit in his 1996 HBR article on strategy—consistency, reinforcing, and optimising. The value chain is not a disparate set of activities. It is a cohesive set of activities, deliberately structured to function as a "system." There must be consistencies among the activities. The activities must not cancel each other out in the results they produce. They need to support and reinforce each other—they function as a tight system so that their total effect is greater than the contribution of each activity. Finally, the activities must have an optimising effect—reducing or eliminating redundancy in the system. This means only performing activities that are absolutely necessary to support the strategy of the company. Porter suggests using an activity-system map to assess the degree of strategic fit in a firm.

Porter argues that strategic fit among value chain activities is necessary not only for strategy but also for sustaining competitive advantage. Rivals can imitate activities but will find it hard to copy an entire activity system of a company. A value proposition supported by a tight activity system is more sustainable. To quote Porter:

> Strategy is creating fit among a company's activities. The success of a strategy depends on doing many things well – not just a few – and integrating among them. If there is no fit among activities, there is no distinctive strategy and little sustainability.[19]

Porter adds, "Fit locks out imitations by creating a chain that is as strong as its strongest link".[20]

Test 3: Trade-Offs

The third test of strategy is trade-offs. "Strategy is making trade-offs in competing. The essence of strategy is choosing what not to do,"[21] says Porter . But, one may ask: Why can't a business serve all customers and all needs? If all businesses serve all customers and all needs, the competition will then be for the best. They will all be competing to be the best, which ultimately will be a race to the bottom, with many going bust and others making poor margins. To make above average profits, companies need to choose the customers and the needs they want to serve. They need to be different from the pack. Targeting customers and customer needs means not serving other customers and other needs. This is a trade-off. Choosing customers and needs to serve also means deciding on products and product features to produce and deliver. This again means not producing other products with other features. This is a trade-off. Once a company has chosen the customers and the specific needs it wants to serve, all decisions and actions of the company have to be consistent and compatible with that choice. Other choices and actions have to be traded-off. For example, it will be inconsistent for the sports car maker Ferrari to go into minivans. It will confuse customers as to what car business Ferrari is in. If Ferrari wants to be a sports car manufacturer, it has to give up on minivans. It has to trade-off to succeed in the sports car business. It cannot produce all cars for all buyers. It will then have no strategy. It will be competing to be the best.

Trade-offs also means deciding what business you are in and, more importantly, what business you are not in. What is your business is a key question in strategy. Strategy involves choosing the industry and market you want to be in. This means not choosing other industries and other markets. This is a trade-off. A business chooses the industry and the market to compete in based on industry and market analysis for profitability and its resources, competencies, and capabilities to compete. There is a tendency for businesses to stray from their core business and go into other businesses. Businesses go after market share and diversification in the belief these will lead to increased revenue and profitability. There is no evidence to support that increased market share leads to increased profitability. It depends on the industry. Smaller firms can be more profitable than larger ones. Diversification through acquisitions or expansion does not guarantee profitability. Often, companies that diversify into other businesses or acquire other businesses come out worse than before. They pay too much for acquisitions or find it difficult to manage a portfolio of businesses. Different businesses require different management expertise and different value chain activities. As a company moves away from its core business, it finds it more and more difficult to succeed. Strategy is about limiting your choice and deciding on your core business. The ability to say no to business opportunities that fall outside your core business is the key to strategy. This is a trade-off the business has to make.

An important reason why companies tend to stray from their core business is the positioning they adopt in the industry. Armstrong and Kotler discuss three positioning errors—under-positioning, over-positioning, and confused positioning.[22] Over-positioning is relevant for our analysis here. Over-positioning occurs when the company presents a too narrow view of its business to customers. This is similar to Levitt's "marketing myopia".[23] Levitt argued that the railroad companies defined their business narrowly as "railroad" rather than more broadly as "transportation". This myopic definition of their business, according to Levitt, was what had prevented railroad companies from expansion and growth. If they had defined their business as transportation, the companies could have expanded into a whole range of businesses that fall within transportation.

While Levitt had a point, marketing myopia has been responsible for the undisciplined expansion of businesses into all kinds of areas far removed from their core business. From a strategic perspective, the problem does not seem to be narrow positioning. On the contrary, the problem is broad and confused positioning where the customer does not know what the business is really about or what value it really offers. The business fails to make the needed trade-off and instead wants it all, with the result the company has no real position in the market.

Finally, trade-offs are necessary because companies need to choose between different strategies to compete in the market. Porter presents three generic strategies for choice—cost, differentiation, and focus.[24] Businesses need to choose one of them. According to Porter, they cannot have them all if they want to avoid "getting stuck in the middle". They need to trade-off.

The need for trade-off in terms of strategic choice arises because of value chain activities. Each of Porter's generic strategy requires a different value chain to support the strategy. The same set of value chain activities cannot support all three generic strategies. Each strategy requires its own value chain. This means, once a business has chosen a particular strategy and developed the supporting value chain activities, it cannot also embrace another strategy because the same value chain activities cannot support two or more different strategies. Each strategy, to be executed, requires its own unique value chain. A business has to make a trade-off, both in its choice of strategy and in its value chain activities.

One area in Porter's strategy that has given rise to controversy and criticism is Porter's insistence that a business has to make a choice about which strategy to follow. It cannot follow more than one strategy without getting stuck in the middle. His critics argue that it is not necessary for a company to lock itself into one strategy—for example, it can adopt a differentiation and cost strategy at the same time. In fact, they argue, it is better for the performance of the company to follow multiple strategies rather than Porter's single strategy. They justify their argument by saying that the business environment has changed today. Companies need to satisfy various customers and different needs. There is more competition now. Companies need more customers and more revenue. Companies need to be flexible, quick, and nimble to take advantage of business opportunities that may appear. Customers want both quality and low cost. In this environment, Porter's single strategy is no longer workable. They call for a blending of different strategies—a "hybrid" strategy. They quote examples of companies that are successful with hybrid strategies. They quote Toyota and IKEA, among others, as companies that have combined differentiation and cost strategies successfully.

The evidence in support of hybrid strategies does not appear to be convincing. To say Toyota and IKEA have hybrid strategies can be misleading. Both compete on the basis of cost. But that does not mean they have no concern for quality. Both strive to meet the minimum quality requirements of customers and give them value. Companies that follow a cost strategy cannot discard quality altogether. They must meet the "threshold" quality expectations of their customers. IKEA gives good design and quality in the house furniture they sell. Toyota is also concerned with quality. It innovates and brings out new models every year. But these activities do not constitute a departure from the dominant strategy of IKEA or Toyota—which is to compete on the basis of cost. Both companies do not over-serve their customers with product features or services because that will take them away from their dominant cost strategy to a differentiation strategy with higher costs.

The mission of IKEA is clear—to serve certain customers who want well designed home furniture at an affordable price. The goal is not to provide exclusive, high quality furniture to the rich. Similarly, Toyota does not think of quality in the way BMW thinks of quality. Toyota's goal is not to offer the quality that BMW offers its customers. Clearly, the competitive strategies of Toyota and BMW are different. For Toyota, it is cost. For BMW, it is differentiation. If one is thinking of a home furniture company that competes on differentiation, it won't be IKEA but a company like Ligne Roset, the French furniture company.

There are examples of companies that have tried what Porter calls "straddling", i.e., blending cost and differentiation strategies. But such attempts have not seen much success. One such company is Continental Airlines. It tried to graft some of the cost features of Southwest into Continental on some of its routes while maintaining itself as a full-service airline on other routes. The straddling strategy failed because Continental's value chain activities could not support a full-service airline and a low-cost carrier. Continental tried to avoid making the needed trade-off, but failed.

JetBlue Airways, a low-cost carrier, attempted to do the opposite of Continental. It tried to incorporate some of the value features of a full-service carrier into its low-cost operations. JetBlue's attempt to combine cost strategy with differentiation strategy has not been a success.

Other examples to straddle include British Airways and McDonald's. British Airways, realising the problems of trade-offs when a business attempts to compete in two ways at the same time, set up a separate subsidiary (Go Fly) to run a low-cost airline. Despite this, the straddling did not work. British Airways concluded that running a low-cost airline was not consistent with its position as a premium airline. It sold its subsidiary.

McDonald's tried to follow Burger King by providing options to customise menus. Customised food preparation affected McDonald's operating costs, service time, and consistency. McDonald's learned that it could not copy Burger King's strategy without affecting its own operations.

Clear positioning is a key to strategy. In the same industry, competitors can hold different positions. In the retail industry, Walmart and Nordstrom compete against each other, but with different strategies. Walmart follows a cost strategy, offering customers "everyday low prices" in rural and semi-urban settings. Nordstrom is an upscale retailer, pursuing a differentiation strategy by offering customers a superior shopping experience in luxury department stores. Target, the third competitor in the retailing world, adopts a straddling position by trying to offer its customers both cost and differentiation benefits. In other words, it tries to compete with Walmart on cost and with Nordstrom on acceptable shopping experience at lower cost. The integration positioning of Target is not easy to sustain. Target is taking a middle ground, where it hopes to create more value for lower cost relative to its two competitors. Managing an integration or hybrid strategy calls for exceptional skills and innovation. Otherwise, the company may end up being "stuck in the middle," as J C Penny discovered in 2011 under Ron Johnson when he tried to change the company's strategic position from a cost leadership to an integration strategy. Rothaermel underscores the point when he says "an integration strategy is actually quite difficult to translate into reality. The reason is that differentiation and cost leadership are distinct strategic positions that require important trade-offs."[25]

A major problem with integration or hybrid strategy is that there is no coherent theory to support it or how to manage it. It merely tries to avoid trade-offs. Porter, on the other hand, provides the theory for why it is necessary to choose a strategic position to compete in an industry and why straddling is hard to do. The theory is built around three elements—industry analysis, positioning, and value chain. There is no similar theoretical foundation for hybrid strategy.

Test 4: Continuity

The fourth test of strategy is continuity. To bear results, there must be continuity in the strategy of a company. Once a company has selected a competitive strategy, it must stick to it until such time when circumstances call for changes in the strategy. Frequent changes in strategy reflect a company's weakness in its positioning. It means it has no clear direction as to how it intends to compete in the market. A strong strategy is one that persists and provides competitive advantage to a company over time. It provides continuity of direction. Continuity of strategy means there is stability in the value proposition the company is making. A consistent pursuit of a selected strategy is essential to exploit its full potential. A strategy can bring results only over time, not immediately. In some cases, it may take ten to fifteen years to successfully execute a strategy. Without strategy continuity, organisations are unlikely to develop competitive advantage.

Continuity of strategy is important for several reasons. Magretta in her book **Understanding Michael Porter** discusses three reasons. First, continuity is essential for a company's identity. Strategy is not just about how a company competes in the market. Strategy is also about creating an image in the mind of the customer—how does the customer perceive the company. A company creates an identity in the market through its strategy—how it positions itself vis-à-vis its competitors. All successful companies occupy certain positions, not only in the market but also in the minds of the customers. The point is underscored by Ries and Trout in their book **Positioning: The Battle for Your Mind** in which they say "positioning is not what you do to a product. Positioning is what you do to the mind of the prospect. That is, you position the product in the mind of the prospect."[26] In other words, companies hold certain positions in the mind of the customer—the customer has a certain mental picture of what a company is about. For a company to create a clear and differentiating identity in the mind of the customer, it needs to present a consistent image of itself to the customer. It can only do this if it has continuity in its strategy—its positioning in the market must be consistent over time. If its positioning keeps shifting, it will only confuse the customer. A confused positioning cannot create an identity for a company in the market that is different from its rivals. Identity is important. Identity gives a company its unique place in the market. It contributes to the company's competitive advantage.

A second reason why continuity of strategy is important is that it helps to build relationships with supply chain partners. In today's environment, companies no longer compete alone. They operate and compete in clusters. Clusters constitute the supply chain partners of a company—suppliers, distributors, retailers, and all those who partner with the company to offer value to the customer. It takes time, effort, and resources to build an effective cluster of partnering companies. If a company keeps shifting its strategy and value proposition, it cannot have the right partners in its cluster. The cluster depends on the strategy of the company. Different strategies require different clusters of partners. For a business to attract a strong cluster of companies around it, it must maintain a clear strategy over time. Clusters are important enablers. They make it possible for a company to compete more effectively. Toyota and Dell will not be able to practice JIT without their cluster of partners. Nestle ensures a steady supply of milk in India through close partnering with local farmers. Similarly, Apple depends on its cluster of partners to produce and deliver its products. Today, competition is between clusters of companies, not between companies. Clusters have replaced vertical integration. Take away the clusters, companies will collapse or will not be able to compete. To build effective partners along the supply chain, companies need to commit to a strategy and direction that persists over time.

The third reason Magretta suggests for continuity in strategy is building an effective value chain. To implement a strategy, an effective value chain is needed. Every strategy needs a unique set of value chain activities to support it. Companies like Southwest, IKEA, and Apple all have their distinctive value chain—hundreds of activities that support the value proposition of the companies. These activities need to be internally consistent and reinforce each another. They need to function as a system to support the strategy a company has adopted. In other words, there must be strategic fit. To build such a support system needs time and resources. This is only possible if there is continuity in the strategy that is being implemented. If there are frequent changes in strategy, an effective value chain cannot be built, which means strategy execution becomes a serious problem. A change in strategy means redoing hundreds of operational activities that have been built over time and replacing them with hundreds of new activities to support the new strategy. This involves changes in organisation, management, human resources, technology, and organisational culture. One can imagine the massive problems frequent changes in strategy can cause an organisation. Frequent changes in strategy can be a serious drag on company performance.

That said, does continuity of strategy mean no change, no innovation? No. Porter himself admits the need for change and innovation in organisations, but insists change is not inconsistent with continuity in strategy. In fact, he believes a consistent strategy will provide the framework for meaningful change and innovation. When we talk about change and innovation, we are mainly talking about change in the value chain activities of a company—changes that will provide greater support to the strategy of the company. Innovation in Southwest or Walmart means reducing cost and adding value in the activities of the company through adoption of best practices—improving Porter's operational effectiveness. The overall goal of OE in the case of Southwest and Walmart is to provide cost-effective support to the value proposition of the companies. Southwest and Walmart continually innovate, but such innovation is guided by the continuity in their strategy, which is to offer a cost-based value proposition to customers. In both companies, their consistent cost-based strategy provides the framework for relevant innovation. Inconsistency in their strategy and value proposition would have made innovation in Southwest and Walmart more difficult or less meaningful. Change and innovation are not antithetical to continuity of strategy. A company needs both continuity and change.

Innovation in organisations need not be confined to Porter's operational effectiveness. It can also be in products and services offered and in the scope and scale of operations. For example, Walmart today is the largest seller of groceries in the United States and sells more DVDs than any other retailer. Despite major changes in its merchandise and store format, Walmart's strategy has remained constant—its value proposition is the same. It continues to offer products at everyday low prices. Magretta quotes another example in her book—India's Aravind Eye Hospital. Since its beginning in 1976, the hospital has grown by leaps and bounds. It now manufactures its own lenses and other consumables used in eye surgery. Aravind's scale and scope of operations have changed dramatically, but its core value proposition has remained constant—to provide affordable eye care. Its expansion, growth, and innovation have all occurred around its primary mission and strategy—to provide eye surgery and eye care to those who cannot afford such services. Its low-cost strategy has guided the hospital in all its operations and innovations.

Does the above discussion mean a company is locked into its strategy and there is no need for strategy change? Are there circumstances that can require a company to review its existing strategy?

Obviously, a company has to revisit its strategy to assess if it is working and producing results. Magretta stresses the point when she says "Continuity of strategy does not mean that an organization should stand still."[27]

There are times when a strategy must be changed—this is referred to as "inflection points" in the strategy literature. Magretta identifies three situations that may call for strategy changes—customer needs, innovation, and technology.

Needs of customers do change for various reasons. New needs arise, old needs become obsolete. Availability of new products and services creates new demands. An example would be new electronic products like mobile phones that did not exist not long ago. Changes in demographics, life-style, and income and educational levels can produce changes in customer needs and wants. Economic and social developments globally have significantly influenced the demand side of business.

The question for strategy is: Is your company strategy still relevant, given the changes on the demand side? Is your company trying to meet a demand that no longer exists or is declining? To avoid getting caught in this kind of situation, it is necessary for a company to periodically assess the relevance and viability of its existing strategy and business model. This calls for asking the famous Drucker's question: "If we weren't already committed to this, is this what we would do?"[28] In other words, would the business be doing what it is doing now if it weren't already in it? Drucker has consistently preached that a business must not hesitate to abandon yesterday. In strategy terms, it means giving up on a strategy that is no longer relevant or working.

Innovation is another situation where a review of strategy is relevant. Innovation in management and value chain activities undermines an existing strategy of a company built around certain trade-offs. The trade-offs may no longer provide the earlier competitive advantage because of innovation in business operations. Dell started with a cost strategy built on certain trade-offs—direct sales and low or zero inventory (built-to-order). Dell enjoyed negative working capital. Dell also concentrated on the business market rather than the consumer market, which fitted well its cost strategy. But the cost advantage provided by Dell's strategy was weakened by innovations in the PC market—outsourcing design and assembly by rivals to low-cost countries, increasing industry sales through retail channels, and growing significance of sales from the consumer market. These changes in the operations of the PC market undermined the cost advantage Dell had enjoyed over the years, forcing Dell to take another look at its long-established strategy. Dell is still grappling with this problem. Michael Dell reflected this concern in the 1990s when he said he was worried about Dell people "who talk about 'the model' as if it were an all-powerful being that will take care of everything. It's scary because I know nothing is ever 100% constant."[29]

A third factor that can trump a company's strategy is technology, in particular disruptive technology. A disruptive technology can make a company's value proposition obsolete. Industry leaders can find their products completely irrelevant to the needs of their customers. This is what happened to Kodak, the dominant producer of photographic film. When digital photography arrived, the leadership position of Kodak was decimated. The impact of technology on undermining current business models can be seen in many industries—including travels, music, newspapers, bookstores, health, and education. But it must be remembered that not all technologies are disruptive or have the same disruptive effect on existing business models. Porter holds the view that truly disruptive technologies are quite rare.

From the above discussion, it is clear that company strategies are not cast in stone. Strategies can and do change. When it is strategic to change strategies they should be changed to deal with new challenges in the competitive environment. Continuity of strategy does not mean continuing to do what is no longer relevant or working. The important question is: Is the strategy working? If it is not working, then it must be changed and a better strategy found. To blindly lock itself into a strategy that was successful in the past but is no longer relevant now will be disastrous for a company. As Drucker reminds us, management must not hesitate to abandon the past. This includes products, practices, processes, and strategies. The need for strategy change becomes more imperative the greater the change in the business environment.

There are many examples of companies that had to change and look for new strategies in order to succeed. These companies started with totally different products from what they are offering now. They struggled and experimented with different business opportunities until they "found" their true business. These companies started small, grew, and learned to compete. They had no clearly defined business or grand strategy when they started. To paraphrase Jim Collins, they tried a lot of stuff and kept what worked.[30]

These "learning companies" include some of the global players in the market today. 3M started as a mining company. Johnson & Johnson had no experience in consumer goods when it began. Marriot had no background in hotels. HP had no experience in the computer business when it launched its first computer product. Disney had no experience with theme park business when it created Disneyland. IBM had no background in electronics when it moved into computers. In the same vein, Boeing had no experience in commercial aircraft business before it went into it.

Nintendo, a market leader in video games, began selling playing cards. It took the company over 60 years to settle on the business it now excels. Facebook's early customers were all college students. It was a change in strategy introduced by Zuckerberg that converted Facebook into the leading social network company that it is today.

Paypal settled on online payment system as a result of change in strategy. Google, when it began, had no clear business model. It only started making money when it radically changed course. YouTube was only successful after it changed its business model. The Gap initially sold records and jeans. It only succeeded after a change in strategy—lower prices, larger selection of store items, and targeting youths.

A classic example of a pivotal change in strategy is Apple. Apple was on the brink of failure in the 1990s. The company had a bewildering array of products, including portable CDs, TV appliances, and digital camera. Steve Jobs reformed it in 1997 and initiated a bold change in direction—focusing on electronics with iMac in 1998. It was a change in strategy, not continuity that was responsible for the success of Apple.

Given the many examples of companies that succeeded only after they changed their products, business models, or strategies, is it meaningful to talk of "continuity" as a hallmark of good strategy? Shouldn't the key word be "flexibility" rather than continuity? Porter disagrees. He argues that "when you substitute flexibility for strategy, your organization never stands for anything or becomes good at anything."[31] Porter is not opposed to flexibility or change. He admits the importance of change, but sees change in the context of strategy. It is strategy that gives direction to change. Change without strategy is purposeless.

It is not possible for a company to commence operations with a full-blown strategy because of uncertainties. Not all the elements of a strategy can be foreseen. Strategy will necessarily evolve over time. In this sense, change is inevitable. But not all change is good or relevant. Change that is relevant is change that strengthens the underlying strategy of the company—its basic value proposition. Without the guidance of strategy, a company may undertake all kinds of change. Some of this change may actually be harmful in that they may weaken the strategy the company is pursuing. Change should strengthen the capacity of the company to better deliver its value proposition. Strategy helps a company to decide what changes are relevant and needed. It is here where continuity of strategy becomes important. If strategies keep changing, it is not possible for them to guide the nature and direction of change that is needed in the organisation.

Porter's view of strategy is dynamic, not static. He admits that strategies cannot be fully designed at the outset. They necessarily evolve and take shape over time. This means change, but change guided by a continuity of strategic direction. Here Porter attempts to reconcile change with continuity. He believes in the importance of continuity in strategy. Continuity gives the company time to understand its strategy and its operations. Strategies become clearer and stronger through a process of discovery and learning over time. The process may sometimes take years to be perfected. Companies like IKEA took decades to fully understand how to implement their strategies. During this period, many changes may be needed to refine the initial value proposition of the company.

At the same time, Porter admits the relevance of change. But what is Porter's understanding of change? Porter adopts a more restrictive view of change in strategy. First, he sees change in the context of operations. Companies must continue to become more efficient and productive. Porter insists companies must remain on the frontier of operational effectiveness. If not, strategy will not matter. This means companies must assimilate best practices in order to retain competitive advantage.

BMW experienced such a situation in the 1990s when it fell behind its rivals in OE improvements. It quickly had to take steps to invest heavily in best practices. BMW learned that it is not enough to have a strategy. The company must not fall behind its competitors in OE.

The second kind of change that Porter considers necessary is related to extending the value proposition of the company or finding better ways to deliver it. In other words, refining the elements of the company strategy or its delivery. These changes are strategy specific.

The important point to bear in mind when Porter talks about change is that he assumes the company already has a strategy. Porter believes flexibility without a consistent strategy will lead to mediocrity. Inflection points calling for fundamental changes in strategy are rare. While industries are dynamic and do change, by and large, industry structures remain stable, according to Porter. This makes it possible for companies to pursue a consistent strategy. Frequent shifts in strategy should be avoided because they are costly to companies. Strategy changes require reconfiguration of value chain activities and realigning entire systems and partner relationships. Frequent shifts in strategy are likely to be a drag on the economic performance of a company.

Porter does not buy the argument that you cannot have continuity because of uncertainty. He says, "Great strategies are rarely, if ever, built on a particularly detailed or concrete prediction of the future."[32] Strategies do not require great predictions or unusual foresight of the future. You only need a broad sense of the future which is often already here, as Drucker was fond of saying. Mulally, the CEO of Ford, once said that strategy is "about a point of view about the future and then making decisions based on that. The worst thing you can do is not have a point of view, and not make decisions."[33] Beyond this fundamental bet about the future, strategy does not require what Porter calls "heroic predictions" about the future. Continuity of strategy is not only desirable but feasible. Whatever change introduced must not conflict with the existing strategy or the trade-offs essential to it. Porter is not talking about changing strategies—he maintains the importance of continuity in strategy and direction. Changes are intended to further define and strengthen the existing strategy—not replace it. Porter does not buy the argument that turbulent and uncertain times call for changes and flexibility in strategy. He argues for the opposite. He thinks, "the deliberate and explicit setting of strategy is more important than ever during periods of change and uncertainty."[34] It is clear strategic direction that can keep companies away from management fads and distractions.

But how do we, then, reconcile Porter's position with those companies that became successful only after they changed their strategies? These companies did not begin with a strategy. They moved away from their initial business into new products and industries. They "tried a lot of stuff" before they found their core business. They virtually stumbled on their core business.

The way to reconcile the two positions is to recognise that Porter, when he talks about strategy, is talking about companies that already have a clear strategic position in the market. He is not discussing companies that are still wandering, looking for businesses or strategies to compete. In his strategy analysis, the experimental stage—trying a lot of stuff—is already over. The entrepreneurial phase has ended. The companies have settled down with their businesses, strategies, and value chains. From this stage, it is continuity of strategy and direction that is important for the performance of the company. Changes, where needed, will be guided by the strategy in place. Too much and unrelated change will be dysfunctional to strategy execution.

Porter's analysis of change and continuity provides the rationale for stability and continued performance in business organisations. Porter's approach to strategy change is incremental. He does not support fundamental changes in strategy. First, he does not believe there is a real need for fundamental changes because industries are largely stable and there are few true inflection points. Second, frequent shifts in strategy will weaken implementation because they will undermine value chain activities that are strategy specific. Consequently, he opts for incremental change.

How legitimate is Porter's position? The strength of Porter's analysis lies in its theoretical foundation—he provides the link between strategy, continuity, change, and value chain. He provides a theory that links all these elements. Those who argue for strategy change and flexibility rarely go beyond providing a pragmatic argument. Strategies need to remain flexible to adapt to changing market and industry conditions. They throw in the argument of technology, innovation, demographics, globalisation, and geopolitics. In short, the business environment is turbulent. In this environment, companies need to remain flexible and be ready to change their strategies and business models to adapt to changing situations. Emphasis on continuity of strategy and business models will be disastrous in the new environment. What worked yesterday is no guarantee it will work tomorrow. The advice of Tom Peters and Waterman to "keep to the knitting"[35] is no longer relevant.

The debate between continuity and change will continue. Companies will experience inflection points, especially in certain industries and countries. Cultural and geopolitical forces will impact transnational companies more in the future. Globalisation will increase instability and turbulence. Given this backdrop, should companies stick to the knitting or abandon yesterday and compete for the future? Or, can they do both? Jim Collins believes it is possible and, in fact, necessary to have both change and continuity.

Falling back on Darwin's theory of evolution, Collins believes successful companies evolve, change, and adapt all the time. This is not only necessary but inevitable because companies are living organisms. They are organic. As living organisms, they evolve and adapt to the changing environment. They mutate through "branching and pruning."[36] Collins says operating practices and business strategies must change constantly in response to a changing world. There is no grand design to which a company can be committed permanently. At the same time, Collins argues successfully that visionary companies retain continuity. The core ideology of the company—its fundamental values and what it stands for—never changes. In Collins' analysis, there is no continuity of strategy, only continuity of values. Strategies can and must change. Values remain constant.

Test 5: Performance

The ultimate test of strategy is performance—is the strategy working? Strategy is intended to enable a company to compete against its rivals. No company can run away from economic performance. It must produce results and there must be clear yardsticks to measure its performance.

Companies use different performance measures. The standard yardstick is financial performance—specifically, return on invested capital (ROIC). Because of certain inherent weaknesses with ROIC as a performance measure, companies are adopting other measurement systems. In recent years, the balanced scorecard has become popular, with its emphasis on measures that go beyond financial returns. Some measure performance using the triple bottom line. How we measure performance is important. But more important is the need to measure performance. Strategies must be evaluated for results. A good strategy is one that produces the desired results—a strategy that works. Strategy is not just about competing. It is about producing superior results. Ultimately, only results count. A successful strategy is one that translates into performance. Intermediary goals—product innovation, customer satisfaction, market share—do not count in the final analysis. That is why ROIC is such a powerful measure of company performance and strategy.

Strategies may not succeed for three reasons. First, the problem may be with the strategy itself. The strategy may not have the capacity to provide any sustainable competitive advantage to the company. The strategy may lack sound strategic thinking and analysis—the strategy is analytically weak. Such a strategy is unlikely to succeed. Second, the strategy may no longer be relevant because of fundamental changes in the competitive environment. The strategy no longer works. This calls for changes to the strategy. Third, the problem may not be with the strategy but with its implementation. The strategy is sound, but it is not working because of poor execution.

It is said the graveyard of strategy is execution. Sound strategies fail because of poor execution. Part of the reason for poor execution is the separation of strategy formulation from strategy implementation. Strategy formulation and strategy implementation are seen as two separate activities, with senior management having responsibility for strategy formulation and the rest of management for strategy execution. This dichotomy explains why many strategies are formulated without any understanding of implementation issues and problems—formulated in a vacuum. Execution problems are not foreseen and built into the strategy at the formulation stage. Strategy formulation cannot be separated from implementation. They are two sides of the same coin. The two need to be integrated right from the beginning. Some strategies, though sound analytically, may not be an option for a company because of lack of execution capabilities—it may not have the needed resources, management expertise, or core competence to execute the strategy successfully. The strategy, though sound, is not feasible for the company. Feasibility is an important constraint to be considered when deciding on a strategy—a good strategy that is not feasible for a company to be carried out is not a good strategy for the company. Fortunately, there are tools today that can help companies to better implement strategies—tools like strategy maps and the balanced scorecard.

It is not always possible to foresee all the problems of implementation when a strategy is formulated. Some of the implementation problems will need to be solved as the strategy gets implemented—they cannot be predicted. But it will be a bad strategy if it does not anticipate implementation problems and take them into account at the point when strategic options are being considered by the company. Reality check is an important component of strategy.

While strategies need to be implementable, one can be too cautious and myopic in strategy development. Too much pessimism can prevent the development of strategic options that are achievable with what Hamel and Prahalad call "stretch." They argue against the notion of "strategic fit", i.e., fit between corporate resources and strategic options. Overemphasis on company resources can become a limiting factor to developing more ambitious strategies. Hamel and Prahalad replace strategic fit with "strategic intent"[37] as the driving force behind bold strategies. The limiting factor is not resources but imagination and boldness to think big, and then move in that direction. Strategic intent is more than mere intention—it is more a state of mind, a device to stretch to achieve what appears, on the surface, to be impossible. It is similar to what Collins and Porras call "BHAGS" in **Built to Last**—Big Hairy Audacious Goals. Think big may, afterall, be more than a slogan.

Notes

1. Henry Mintzberg and James Quinn [1].
2. Michael Porter [2].
3. **Ibid.**, pp. 61–63.
4. **Ibid.**, p. 62.

5. **Ibid.**, p. 62.
6. **Ibid.**, p. 61.
7. Michael Porter [3].
8. Joan Magretta [4].
9. Michael Porter [5].
10. **Ibid.**, p. 223.
11. **Ibid.**, p. 223.
12. **Ibid.**, p. 227.
13. The discussion that follows is based on the analysis of Joan Magretta. See her **Understanding Michael Porter** (Harvard Business Review Press, 2012), pp. 93–94 and Chaps. 4–7.
14. Peter Drucker [6].
15. Michael Porter [7].
16. Joan Magretta, **op. cit**. See Chap. 4, "Creating Value".
17. Joan Magretta, **op. cit**., p. 106.
18. Michael Porter [8].
19. Michael Porter [9].
20. **Ibid.**, p. 70.
21. **Ibid.**, p. 70.
22. See Gary Armstrong and Philip Kotler [10].
23. Theodore Levitt [11].
24. Michael Porter [12].
25. Frank Rothaermel [13].
26. Al Ries and Jack Trout [14].
27. Joan Margretta, **op. cit**., p. 165.
28. Quoted in William Cohen [15].
29. Quoted in Joan Margretta, **op. cit**., p. 171.
30. See James Collins and Jerry Porras [16].
31. Quoted in Joan Margretta, **op. cit**., p. 172.
32. Quoted in Joan Margretta, **op. cit**., p. 168.
33. Quoted in Joan Margretta, **op. cit**., p. 169.
34. See Joan Margretta, **op. cit**., pp. 181–182.
35. Tom Peters and Robert Waterman [17].
36. See James Collins and Jerry Porras [18].
37. See Hamel and Prahalad [19].

References

1. Mintzberg H, Quinn J (1996) The strategy process, 3rd ed. Prentice Hall, pp 10–15
2. Porter M (1996) What is strategy?. Harvard Business Review, p 63
3. Porter M (1980) Competitive strategy. The Free Press, p 148
4. Magretta J (2012) Understanding michael porter. Harvard Business Review Press, p 27
5. Porter M (1985) Competitive advantage. The Free Press, p 221

6. Drucker P (2001) The essential drucker. Collins Business, p 20
7. Porter M (1996) What is strategy?. Harvard Business Review, p 60
8. Porter M (1985) Competitive advantage. The Free Press, p 37
9. Porter M (1996) What is strategy?" Harvard Business Review, p 75
10. Armstrong G, Kotler P (2003) Marketing: an introduction, 6th ed. Prentice Hall, p 263
11. Levitt T (1960) Marketing myopia. Harvard Business Review
12. Porter M (1980) Competitive strategy. The Free Press, p 35
13. Rothaermel F (2013) Strategic management. McGraw-Hill Irwin, p 159
14. Ries A, Trout J (2001) Positioning: the battle for your mind. McGraw-Hill, p 2
15. Cohen W (2010) Drucker on leadership. Jossey-Boss, p 27
16. Collins J, Porras J (2002) Built to last. Harper Business Essentials
17. Peters T, Waterman R (1982) In search of excellence. Harper Collins Business
18. Collins J, Porras J (2002) Built to last. Harper Business Essentials, p 152
19. Hamel G, Prahalad CK (1989) Strategic intent. Harvard Business Review

Chapter 2
Strategy Making and Implementing

Abstract This chapter explores deeper into the meaning of strategy through the theme 'Strategy Making and Implementing'. Specifically, it focuses on strategic thinking, strategic analysis, and strategic planning. Major works on these concepts are reviewed and assessed, including the contributions of Ohmae, Hamel and Prahalad, Mintzberg, and Rumelt. Asian and Western modes of thinking are noted. The impact of values and beliefs on strategic thinking and analysis is discussed. The decision making process and the limitations of rational decision making are explored. Do strategies come from strategic planning or 'emerge' is examined. Implementation is the graveyard of strategies. The problems in strategy implementation are reviewed, with particular reference to Porter, Mintzberg, and Kim and Mauborgne. Challenges like whether strategic thinking can be modelled and taught is also taken up. Together with Chap. 1, the parameters of strategy become clearer. The confusion and consensus in the understanding of strategy become more apparent.

There are three concepts in strategy that cause much confusion—strategic thinking, strategic analysis, and strategic planning. What is the relationship between these concepts? How is strategy related to them? How does strategy get formed? These are important questions if we want to understand what processes are involved in strategy making.

Strategic Thinking and Strategic Analysis

For some, strategies do not come from rigorous analysis but from a thought process that is creative and intuitive, not rational. In other words, it is strategic thinking that matters, not strategic analysis. Keniche Ohmae, the leading Japanese strategy guru, points out that many Japanese strategists who founded global companies had little formal education and training in strategic analysis. What they had was "an intuitive grasp of the basic elements of strategy… an idiosyncratic mode of thinking."[1] In other words, they had a "strategic mind" that could "see" business opportunities and how to convert them into successful ventures. It is insight and creativity that explains their

© The Author(s), under exclusive license to Springer Nature Singapore Pte Ltd. 2021

L. Iruthayasamy, *Understanding Business Strategy*,
https://doi.org/10.1007/978-981-33-6542-1_2

success—not training in strategic analysis. In fact strategic analysis is likely to drive away strategic thinking. To Ohmae, strategic thinking is an art—which means it is difficult to organise and programme the process. It is essentially intuitive judgment. It is a way of thinking, a habit of analysis. The strategic mind possesses an "intellectual elasticity or flexibility" that enables the strategist to come up with realistic solutions to challenges. Ohmae goes on to stress that "successful business strategies result not from rigorous analysis but from a particular state of mind."[2] Strategy is the result of a "thought process that is basically creative and intuitive rather than rational."[3] Ohmae concedes that strategists do not reject analysis, but they use it only to stimulate the creative process. Great strategies "originate in insights that are beyond the reach of conscious analysis."[4]

If strategy is the result of some spark, intuition, or insight in the mind of the strategist, does it follow that strategic thinking cannot be learned? Ohmae believes creativity cannot be taught, but it can be learned. There are certain things we can do to stimulate the creative process in our minds. Strategic success cannot be reduced to a formula. However, "there are habits of mind and modes of thinking that can be acquired through practice"[5] to help free the creative power within us to come up with winning strategies.

Kenichi Ohmae believes it is possible to marshal the thinking process and develop the habits of mind and modes of thinking needed for strategic thinking. In his book **The Mind of the Strategist** Ohmae discusses three kinds of thinking—mechanical systems thinking, intuition, and strategic thinking. Systems thinking is logical, vertical, analytical. Intuitive thinking is more feeling, sensing, insight-driven. Strategic thinking is creative problem solving—the ability to take things apart and put them back in new combinations and patterns. It is a combination of rational analysis and imagination. Strategic thinking is nonlinear thinking, but at the same time it is not just intuition—reaching conclusions without analysis. For Ohmae, strategic thinking is linked to analysis. The two are complementary. He puts it like this:

> For strategic mind to work creatively, it needs the stimulus of a good, insightful analysis. In order to conduct a good analysis, it takes a strategic and inquisitive mind to come up with the right questions and phrase them as solution-oriented issues… Intuition or gut-feel alone does not ensure secure business plans. It takes a good balance between the two to come up with a successful strategy.[6]

To Ohmae, there is a process and method to strategic thinking, not the linear process of systems analysis but a broader, more focused approach to looking at problems and solutions. The habits of mind and modes of thinking needed for strategic thinking can be learned and applied to problem analysis. This is in line with recent trends in teaching thinking courses in universities and training managers in brain games to improve their capacity for creative problem solving. It appears that mind games and problem-solving activities are particularly effective tools for developing strategic thinking skills. Chess and Go, the strategic board game of China, Japan, and Korea, have shown to be beneficial. Harold Henkel in his article "Can Strategic Thinking Be Taught?" differentiates chess from Go and points out that the latter is a game of patience, balance, and judgment. "Winning consists not in destroying one's opponent, but in achieving a comparative advantage."[7] While chess is principally a game of tactics, Go is a game of strategy. It teaches strategic thinking and judgment.

In his paper, Henke l cites the work of Andrew Watson and Sangit Chatterjee on Go. Watson and Chatterjee advocate Go as an effective tool for management learning, specifically in three areas: (1) formulation of international strategy, (2) entry into foreign markets, and (3) resource allocation. According to them, Go teaches how to balance the competing claims of local tactics with global strategy.

Kenichi Ohmae begins his book **The Mind of the Strategist** with "Analysis is the critical starting point of strategic thinking."[8] Faced with problem situations, the strategic thinker "dissects them into their constituent parts. Then, having discussed the significance of these constituents, he reassembles them in a way calculated to maximise his advantage."[9] This is in line with Ohmae's concept of strategy. The "object of strategy is to bring about the conditions most favourable to one's own side."[10]

To Ohmae, strategic thinking calls for a particular method of thinking, employing certain analytical tools. He discusses several strategic thinking tools in his book, which include:

- Issue diagram
- Profit diagram
- Key factors for success (KFS)
- Strategic degrees of freedom
- Building on relative superiority
- Strategic triangle.

Apart from the above, Ohmae provides a host of other ideas to guide the strategic thinking process. While Ohmae separates strategic thinking from strategic analysis, he stresses the need to guide strategic thinking through relevant analytical tools. He realises that strategic thinking is not possible in a vacuum—you need concepts, theories, models, and frameworks to think strategically. In other words, strategic thinking cannot be decoupled from strategic analysis.

If strategic thinking is not "free" thinking but is guided by analytical tools, can we model the strategic thinking process? If we can model the process, we can teach and train managers to think strategically.

There are attempts to do this. Jeanne Liedtka in her article "Strategic Thinking: Can it be Taught?" identifies five elements of strategic thinking[11]:

- Systems perspective
- Intent-focused
- Intelligent opportunism
- Thinking in time
- Hypothesis-driven.

The strategic thinker thinks in terms of "systems". He "has a mental model of the complete end-to-end system of value creation, and understands the interdependencies within it."[12] The mental model of how the world works incorporates both the external and the internal context of the organization. Problems and challenges

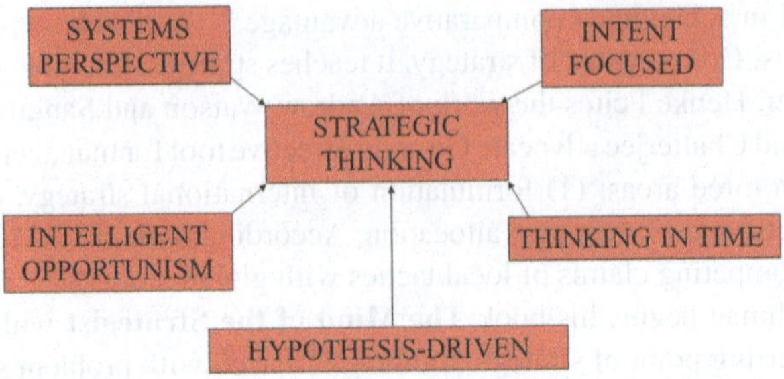

Fig. 2.1 The elements of strategic thinking. *Source* Liedtka [3, p. 122]

are seen in systemic terms. The strategic thinker sees the connections and linkages within the system and appreciates that most organisational problems are systems problems. He understands the relationship (fit) between the corporate, business, and functional levels of strategy. He also understands the connections across departments and functions, including between suppliers and buyers (Fig. 2.1).

Strategic thinking is intent-focused and intent-driven. The concept of strategic intent comes from Hamel and Prahala d. In their book **Competing For The Future**, they describe it as the dream that energises a company and provides the emotional and intellectual fire for it.[13] The paragraph that follows draws heavily from the book.

Strategic intent implies a significant stretch for the organisation. Current capabilities and resources are manifestly insufficient to the task. Strategic intent also implies a particular point of view about the long-term market or competitive position that a firm hopes to build over the coming decade or so. Hence, it conveys a sense of direction. A strategic intent is differentiated. It implies a competitively unique point of view about the future. It holds out to employees the promise of exploring a new competitive territory. It conveys a sense of discovery. Strategic intent has an emotional edge to it. It is a goal that employees perceive as inherently worthwhile. Hence, it implies a sense of destiny. Direction, discovery, and destiny—these are the attributes of a strategic intent. Strategic thinking is concerned with and driven by the continuous reshaping of strategic intent.

Strategic intent "provides the focus that allows individuals within an organisation to marshal and leverage their energy, to focus attention, to resist distraction, and to concentrate for as long as it takes to achieve a goal."[14]

The third element of strategic thinking is intelligent opportunism. The "essence of the notion is the idea of openness to new experience which allows one to take advantage of alternative strategies that may emerge as more relevant to a rapidly changing business environment."[15] This is Mintzberg's emergent strategy. In practising intelligent opportunism, organisations should consider inputs from employees lower down the organisation. It should not be just top-down strategy but also emergent strategy from below. If you want to create a point of view about the future of the organisation, you need the participation of everyone in the organisation. Grand strategies that are "nice and clear" preclude the majority of people in the organisation from having any impact on strategy. Mintzberg puts it like this:

> You've precluded 99 percent of the people in the organisation from having any impact on strategy... And so a healthy strategy system in any company is one in which there is a tremendous amount of communication and interaction around ideas and possibilities – from the ground, from middle management, from senior management – weaving back and forth, in and out."[16]

In an interview with the magazine **Across the Board** in 1999, Mintzberg said, "Strategy is something that gets shaped and changed and adjusted as you go along. It's not some magic formula."[17]

The fourth element of strategic thinking is "thinking in time". Thinking in time is connecting the past with the present and the future. Strategic thinking is always thinking in time. Neustadt and May state:

> Thinking in time (has) three components. One is recognition that the future has no place to come from but the past, hence the past has predictive value. Another is recognition that what matters for the future in the present is departures from the past, alterations, changes, which prospectively or actually divert familiar flows from accustomed channels... A third component is continuous comparison, an almost constant oscillation from the present to future to past and back, heedful of prospective change, concerned to expedite, limit, guide, counter or accept it as the fruits of such comparison suggest.[18]

In short, strategic thinking connects the past, present, and the future. It uses an organisation's memory and history as critical inputs for creating its future. There is a sense of continuity with the past and a sense of direction for the future. This is necessary to maintain a feeling of control in the midst of change. Strategy is driven not by future intent alone. "It is the gap between today's reality and that intent for the future that is critical."[19]

The fifth element in strategic thinking is recognising it as a "hypothesis-driven" process, i.e., hypotheses generation and testing as core activities. The ability to develop good hypotheses and to test them are critical to strategic thinking. As the future is unknowable, it is necessary to proceed on the basis of some judgments about what we think is going to happen, collect the data, and test them. Strategic thinking is both creative and critical. It avoids the analytic-intuitive dichotomy in thinking.

Taken together, these five elements create a capacity for strategic thinking, according to Liedtka. Enhancing the strategic thinking skills of individuals in the organisation enhances the strategy-making capability of the organisation.

Others too have proposed formalised approaches to strategic thinking. For example, Zabriskie and Huellmantel present a sequential six-step process to strategic thinking.[20] Still others talk about the habits of the strategic thinker. Basically, these theorists believe strategic thinking is really analytical thinking. Porter reflects this school when he says:

> Strategic thinking involves asking two critical questions. First, what is the structure of your industry, and how it is likely to evolve over time?.... Second, what is your company's relative position in the industry?[21]

Porter uses the term "strategic thinking" to mean strategic planning—an analytical process, not a synthetic and divergent process as viewed by Ohmae and Mintzberg.

The question for strategy is: Is it functional to attempt to model the strategic thinking process? To model the process is not just to understand how strategic thinking takes place but to prescribe how to think strategically. Any such prescription is likely to be more dysfunctional than functional.

While we need analytical tools to think strategically, the thinking process itself can never be understood precisely because so much of it is intuitive and perceptual, related to the personality of the strategic thinker and the context of the problem. Studies by psychologists like Carl Jung clearly show that different people think, analyse, and decide differently. People gather information differently—by sensation or intuition, but not by both. They evaluate information by thinking or feeling. Individuals solve problems and make decisions in different ways—by sensation, intuition, thinking, or feeling. The Myer-Briggs personality assessments show sixteen different types of personalities. This means sixteen different perceptions, mindsets, and behaviours.[22] This is a major reason for divergence in strategic thinking and why, when faced with a common strategic problem, different people come up with different strategies to tackle the challenge.

More importantly, this divergence in thinking and problem solving is critical to sound strategy formulation. It is only divergent thinking that can produce strategies that are different from existing ones, which is the key test of a successful strategy. It is divergent thinking that can produce change and innovation in organisations, not convergent thinking. Change and innovation are intimately linked to strategy. This explains why global companies today embrace diversity in their workplace—including employing more women and empowering them. Diversity is a major source of creativity and innovation, which is so essential for building effective competitive strategies. Any attempt to prescribe how to think strategically—to model the process—may not serve the cause of strategy.

Strategic thinking is essentially an intuitive and subconscious process. It can be guided by analytical tools to help the mind focus on certain essential elements, but it is separate from strategic analysis. On the contrary, it guides strategic analysis by providing hypotheses about how to solve specific problems. The hypotheses are then tested by analysis for validity. If accepted, the hypotheses become strategies. The relationship between strategic thinking and strategic analysis is interactive. The seeds for analysis and strategy come from strategic thinking. This is in line with the notion that strategy is a hypothesis. Richard Rumelt, an eminent strategy guru, draws a parallel between hypothesis in science and strategy. He says:

> "In science, a new idea or theory is a called a hypothesis… The new theory cannot have been deduced from existing knowledge, else it wouldn't be new! It arises as an insight or creative judgment… A strategy is, like a scientific hypothesis, an educated prediction of how the world works."[23]

Strategy, as a hypothesis, comes from strategic thinking, which is then refined and reformulated through analysis and planning. Research indicates there are different kinds of intelligence. Similarly, there are different kinds of thinking. Ohmae talks about three kinds of thinking. Others talk about vertical versus lateral thinking. Still others talk about left-brain and right-brain thinking. Left-brain thinking is vertical, logical, while right-brain thinking is inductive, lateral, and holistic. Women are said to be more right-brained thinkers, while men are left-brained thinkers. Women are wired differently from men. This has important implications for problem solving. The research of Edward de Bono on different thinking styles and his famous six thinking hats reinforces the point that people think differently. We live in a perceptual world. We act on the basis of perception, not reality. Perceptual reality limits the value of analysis in problem solving and decision making.

In 1947 Herbert Simon raised the issue of rational analysis in his book **Administrative Behavior** and concluded that there is no absolute rationality, only "bounded rationality." All decisions are premised not on facts alone but also on values. And values are related to the decision maker. Different decision makers have different values, which means the way they perceive and analyse problems, evaluate alternative polices, and arrive at solutions is different. Analysis is not an objective exercise, independent of the analyst. Analytical models, like Porter's Five Forces, can lead to different strategy choices, depending on who is doing the analysis and his value premises. Same analysis need not result in same strategies. Different strategy outcomes are possible.

Different strategic minds operating with different perceptions, values, and belief systems can result in different strategies for the same problem or challenge. For example, an Islamic or Confucian manager employing Porter's industry analysis may opt for different strategic choices from a Western analyst because of differences in values and belief systems. A manager wanting to restructure an Islamic bank will consider analysis and strategy options that are "shariah" compliant. His thinking, analysis, and choices will be different from a banker given the same task for a non-Islamic bank. A capitalist and a socialist will make different strategy choices given the same problem. Different values, beliefs, and thinking processes greatly influence strategic analysis and strategy choices. The literature on strategic management is weak on value inputs for strategy formulation. There is inadequate emphasis on the "geography of thought" and its impact on strategy.

Richard Nisbett in his book **The Geography of Thought** shows how the West and East think differently—there are major cognitive differences between the two. Asians see the world differently—they think holistically. Westerners think analytically and logically. Asians can entertain contradictory propositions at the same time—dialectical reasoning. Westerners find this illogical. In short, Asians and Westerners have different modes of thinking and values. Cross-cultural studies by people like Hofstede, Laurent, Trompenaars, and Hampden-Turner show that countries differ in culture and people in different cultures interpret and respond to the same strategic challenges in different ways.[24]

This is particularly evident in international business in such strategic decisions as choice of countries to enter, mode of entry, ownership, acquisitions, mergers, risk avoidance, and time horizon. In international strategy, cultural distance is often more important than physical distance. Countries prefer to do business with other countries that are similar in culture, ideology, and institutional framework. Capitalism itself is an ideology, with its own distinctive perspective on competition and the purpose of business. Strategic thinking and analysis developed within the precepts of capitalism need not be similar to those developed in a socialist, Confucian, or Islamic society. Other forms of strategic thinking and analysis based on different values and goals can be equally valid. In other words, there is no one best way to think, analyse, and formulate strategies. There is no one best strategy either to deal with a problem. Strategy is a hypothesis—an experimental solution to a problem that provides an opportunity to learn, refine, and improve as we go along. Rarely is it a best solution to a problem. To become a successful strategy, the hypothesis must create enough discord and discussion or, in the words of Richard Pascale, "constructive contention." It is the constructive contention that converts the hypothesis into a working strategy.

Strategic thinking and strategic analysis are closely linked to decision making and problem solving. How are organisational decisions made? What is the managerial decision making process? There are three principal decision making models:

- Rational Comprehensive
- Satisficing
- Incremental.

The rational comprehensive model sees problem analysis and decision making as a process that is comprehensive and rational. Decision problems are precisely identified, their causes established, the full range of alternative solutions and their consequences weighed using cost-benefit analysis, and the best course of action or policy selected based on maximising benefits. This analytical and decision model, while ideal, offers little help to the manager interested in strategies or policies for specific challenges. The model is neither normative nor descriptive. Its analytical demands are too high, making the model impractical for decision makers. The strategist facing a problem does not have the luxury of unlimited analysis. He needs to decide and move forward, facing the consequences of his choice subsequently. A not-so-good decision taken timely is better than a good decision taken too late. Timing is crucial in strategic decisions. Too much analysis often leads to paralysis. It is action that counts. Reflection is important and necessary, but is only an input for strategy. It is not the objective of the process.

The limitation of the rational comprehensive model as an analytical tool for decision making and problem solving led Herbert Simon to suggest an alternative—the "satisficing model." The merit of this model is that it simplifies the decision process by reducing the demand for analysis and information. It does not recommend that the decision maker or strategist go for the "best" decision but for the "good enough" choice—a choice that satisfies the decision criteria of the decision maker. The decision made or strategy chosen may not be the best, but it meets the minimum criteria as decided by the policy or decision maker. The strategy or decision is good enough, given the constraints of the situation. The satisficing model, by reducing the complexity of the analytical process, offers the decision maker or the strategist a way of thinking and analysing a problem that is administratively feasible. It meets the action needs of the problem solver. The model, consequently, is relevant for strategic thinking and strategic analysis. Kenichi Ohmae's KFS (key factors for success) is an application of Simon's model. The strategic mind focuses. It is not comprehensive. It focuses on the few, key things that matter—those things that are likely to determine the success or failure of a strategic move.

The incremental model is similar to Simon's satisficing in that it also simplifies the decision process by reducing the demands placed on the decision maker for analysis and information. But its methodology is different from Simon's approach. The roots of the incremental model go back to 1959 to an article written by Charles Lindblom called **The Science of "Muddling Through"**.[25] Lindblom dismissed the rational comprehensive description of analysis in decision and policy making as unrealistic. The model is too demanding in terms of information required and analysis needed. It is also too risky for the policy maker, as he cannot predict the future consequences of his decisions. The farther he moves from existing strategies and policies the greater the risk he takes should his decisions turn out to be wrong. The policy maker, especially in the public sector, is conservative and risk averse. He wants change but at the same time he wants to play it safe. Any fundamental departure from existing practices and policies increases his risk. To reduce this risk, the decision maker prefers policy changes to be incremental—only marginally different from existing policies. In this way, he brings changes in small steps. This enables him to monitor and control the change process better. It also reduces the amount of analysis needed for strategic choice. The process also reduces risk because change is incremental. If the decision maker makes a wrong decision, he can always rectify it because an incremental change, if it goes wrong, is unlikely to cause too much damage to the organisation. Although the process appears to be "muddling through", Lindblom argued there is a method in it—that is why he called it a "science" of muddling through.

The incremental decision model has remained prominent in the literature on strategy. Its more recent champion is James Quinn. His "logical incrementalism" is built on Lindblom's ideas of incremental change. Logical incrementalism is a reaction to planned strategy, with its emphasis on comprehensive analysis and fundamental strategic choices. Quinn's ideas are closer to Mintzberg than Porter, with a bias for a more ad hoc and emergent approach to strategy. Strategy need not be a quantum change, planned and executed from the top. It can be small changes taking place at all levels in the organisation. Quinn has this to say on planning:

> My data suggests that when well-managed major organizations make significant changes in strategy, the approaches they use frequently bear little resemblance to the rational, analytical systems so often described in the planning literature.[26]

Quinn adds that most planning is carried out bottom-up and is "intended only as frameworks to guide and provide consistency for future decisions made incrementally during shorter term operating cycles."[27]

The three decision models discussed underscore the point that there is more than one way to think about a problem or find solutions. There is no one best way to analyse a problem or one best solution to a problem. The analytical and solution-seeking process is creative. In this sense, strategy cannot be taught. The tools of strategy can be taught. You need a creative mind or a collection of creative minds to use the strategic tools to come up with a strategy that is better than that of your competitors.

Strategic Planning

The above discussion has been on strategic thinking and analysis. How does strategy and strategic planning fit in this discussion?

There is no consensus in the literature on the relationship between strategic thinking and strategic planning. There are two viewpoints. The Porter view is that strategic thinking is analytical thinking, and part of strategic planning. In strategic planning, analytical tools are used to aid strategic thinking. To Porter, there is no separation between strategic thinking, analysis, planning, and strategy. Strategy is the result of strategic analysis and planning.

The second view is championed by Mintzberg. To him, strategic thinking and strategic planning are distinct thinking modes. Strategic thinking precedes strategic planning. This view holds that planning cannot produce strategies. Planning is the programming of strategies. Planning is what happens after strategies have been selected or have emerged.

Mintzberg attacks strategic planning by arguing that it is based on fallacies.[28] He points out three fallacies—the fallacy of prediction, the fallacy of detachment, and the fallacy of formalisation. Planning requires predicting what will happen in the future, which is not possible. Detachment involves the premise that strategies can be produced through formalised procedures by planners detached from operations. Formalisation is concerned with the idea that strategies can result from formalised procedures. To Mintzberg, formalised procedures are productive only in terms of operationalising already existing strategies. The emphasis of this view is that strategic thinking and strategic planning are different. Strategic thinking is synthetic and divergent, whereas strategic planning is analytical and convergent. The true role of strategic planning is the operationalisation of existing strategies, not the generation of new strategies. Planning cannot generate new strategies. It can only programme them. Some even take the extreme position that strategic planning is useless and should be scrapped in favour of strategic thinking.[29] Fundamentally, Mintzberg emphasises the creative and synthetic in strategy, while Porter emphasises the convergent and analytic. Mintzberg is concerned with how strategies are arrived at in organisations. Porter is concerned with how organisations position themselves in an industry for competitive advantage and superior performance.

Mintzberg concedes that strategic planning is not dead, but adds that strategic planning often spoils strategic thinking. To Mintzberg, "Planners should make their greatest contribution around the strategy-making process rather than inside it."[30] That is, planners should supply the formal analyses and the hard data needed for strategy making. Planners act as catalysts to support strategy making by aiding and helping managers to think strategically. They are programmers of strategy—formulating the details of strategy implementation. In this way, Mintzberg separates strategic thinking from strategic planning, but, at the same time, shows the link between the two and how they complement each other.

Mintzberg is not happy to hand over strategy making to planners. He fears that planners will formalise the process and kill strategic thinking along the way. He believes the strategy-making process must be free if it is to be creative and innovative. He stresses:

> Strategies often cannot be developed on schedule and immaculately conceived. They must be free to appear at any time and at any place in the organization, typically through messy processes of informal learning that must necessarily be carried out by people at various levels who are deeply involved with the specific issues at hand.[31]

The above is in line with Drucker's thinking that "planning as the term is commonly understood is actually incompatible with an entrepreneurial society and economy" and that "innovation, almost by definition has to be decentralized, ad hoc, autonomous, and micro-economic."[32]

It must be emphasised that Mintzberg does not reject strategic planning. He only differs in the role planners can play in the strategy-making process, which is different from the conventional wisdom found in the literature on strategic management. He accepts planning, plans, and planners as relevant to strategy. But he redefines the role of planners. Planners are not strategy makers. They are only strategy programmers. Planners provide the analyses needed for strategic thinking. Mintzberg stresses that "strategies cannot be created by analysis, but their development can be helped by it."[33] Planning plays a critical role in programming strategies and making them operational. Plans are needed to communicate, control, and coordinate. Plans in the form of programmes, schedules, budgets, and so on are management tools for strategy execution. They are also needed to convince external stakeholders, like financiers and partners, about the intentions and purpose of the organisation.

The fundamental position of Mintzberg is that one must not confuse planning with strategy making. Planners do not make strategies, they make plans. Strategies are made or should be made by managers. Planners provide the analysis needed by managers for strategy making. Planners are good at analytical thinking, but they must not "enter the black box of strategy making". They must "ensure that the box is occupied with active line managers."[34] In other words, planners make it possible for managers to think creatively. The role of planners and managers is complementary. Planners can be catalysts and even strategy finders, but their function is not strategy making. They can help identify emergent strategies and stimulate learning within the organisation. Planning is learning, as pointed out by Geus in his 1988 HBR article "Planning as Learning" in which he said, "the real purpose of effective planning is not to make plans but to change the… mental models that … decision makers carry in their heads."[35] Planning must be distinguished from strategising. Gary Hamel puts it in his unique style: "Giving planners responsibility for creating strategy is like asking a bricklayer to create Michelangelo's Pieta."[36] The relationship between

Fig. 2.2 Strategic thinking and strategic planning. *Source* Heracleous [8, p. 485]

strategic thinking and strategic planning is captured by Heracleous in the diagram below (Fig. 2.2).

But how are strategies actually made then? How do they come into being? There are two views on this. The planning view is that strategies are deliberate. They are the result of strategic planning—the end product of the planning process. The second view is that strategies largely emerge from within the organization—they are not planned. Both views have their strong advocates. Porter supports the planning school. Mintzberg is for the emergent perspective.

The planning school of strategy is the traditional school—going back to Ansoff and his 1965 book on corporate strategy.[37] This approach to strategy making is prescriptive. A series of logical and sequential steps are advocated to arrive at the best strategy. The process includes:

- External audit—examining the competitive environment (including the wider macro-environment) for opportunities and threats
- Internal audit—examining the strengths and weaknesses of the organisation compared to competitors
- SWOT analysis—examining the "fit" between the external and internal environments
- Identification and evaluation of alternative strategies to achieve the objectives and mission of the organisation
- Selection of the "best" strategy
- Implementation of the strategy through resources and operational systems, including controlling through monitoring mechanisms.

Here strategy is a "plan", arrived at through a planning process that optimises rational choice. In the planning approach, strategy is formulated through systematic analysis using tools such as industry analysis, portfolio matrix, core competence, etc. It is the product of strategic analysis that is top-down (the CEO is regarded as the chief strategist). There is separation between strategy formulation and strategy execution. In this respect, it is similar to Taylor's separation between thinking and doing. Planners and top management formulate strategy. Middle management and the rest in the organisation implemented strategy. Sophisticated frameworks and tools are deployed to assist strategy formulation and execution.

Within the planning approach, there are distinct perspectives. Porter focuses on industry analysis and positioning. Barney focuses on unique organisational resources and core competencies. Pheng emphasise formal and informal institutions as key determinants of strategy. Kim and Mauborgne in blue ocean strategy focus on strategic moves that make competition irrelevant. But they all share a common position on strategy—i.e., strategy is deliberate and is formulated on the basis of analysis, though the focus of analysis maybe different.

A contrary concept of strategy making is championed by Mintzberg.[38] His approach to strategy is characterised by the following:

- Strategic planning does not and cannot produce strategies. Strategies come from strategic thinking. Strategic planning is not strategic thinking. Strategic planning spoils strategic thinking. Strategic planning relies on analysis. Strategic thinking relies on synthesis. Strategy making is a synthesising process. The term strategic planning is an oxymoron.
- Role of strategic planning is not to produce strategies but to programme strategies that already exist. Strategic planning converts existing strategies into programmes, action plans, activities, and schedules to be implemented.
- Strategic planning involves three steps:
  - Coding or calibrating the strategy. The strategy is clarified and expressed to render it operational. All implicit assumptions are made explicit. Planning "brings order to strategy."
  - Elaborating the strategy. The strategy is decomposed into sub-strategies and specific action plans—what needs to be done to realise the intended strategy.
  - Converting the elaborated strategy. This is converting the strategy into organisational routines and operations, such as objectives, budgets, policies, and standard operating procedures. This is detailed programming of strategy for execution and performance control.

- Strategic plans are meant for strategy execution, not strategy formulation. Strategies get formed within the organisation through an ad hoc, grass-root process of productive learning or "double-loop"[39] learning, to use Argyris's words. Strategies "emerge" within the organisation through learning and action processes. The emergent strategies are then "programmed"—defined, clarified, and operationalised in the strategic plan for implementation purposes. The informal, emergent strategies get recognised as formal strategies of the organisation through strategic planning.

- Strategies can be deliberate or emergent. Emergent strategies "develop inadvertently, without the conscious intention of senior management." They are not conceived or developed on schedule. They can "appear at any time and at any place in the organization, typically through messy processes of informal learning…"[40] This is grass-roots strategy making. "Strategies grow like weeds in a garden." These become organisational when they develop into "patterns" of actions. Top management may "guide" the development of such patterns through deploying "umbrella strategies" which set broad policy parameters for strategies to emerge in the organisation. The function of management is to "create the climate within which a wide variety of strategies can grow." This includes building flexible structures, hiring creative people, formulating umbrella strategies, and recognising patterns that emerge. "Effective strategies can show up in the strangest places and develop through the most unexpected means. There is no one best way to make strategy."[41]
- Deliberate strategies are the product of strategic thinking, which are then programmed through strategic planning. Emergent strategies are not deliberate—they are patterns of action that emerge over time within an organisation. They get recognised and programmed as formal strategies of the organisation. Strategies can be plans for the future or patterns from the past. Strategies can be formulated or can form. The advantage of emergent strategy (strategy that forms) is that it is the product of learning. Purely deliberate strategy is formulated—it separates thinking from doing. Strategy as pattern fosters learning. There is no separation between formulation and implementation. Strategy forms gradually, through the actions and experiences of the organisation. Mintzberg uses the metaphor of "crafting" to describe such a strategy making process, which implies that the process is more intuitive than rational, more experiential. Strategy formulation and implementation is one process, each feeding into the other. It is experimental, action, and learning. It is similar to Whittington's perspective of strategy as "practice."[42]

Strategy Implementing

It is obvious that implementing strategy is critically linked to the strategy making process. The literature on strategy implementation shows that well over 50% of strategies do not get implemented. To quote Sull et al., "Studies have found that two-thirds to three-quarters of large organisations struggle to implement their strategies."[43] In other words, only a small percentage of strategic intents and objectives get realised. Many strategies fail not because the strategies are bad but because the implementation is bad. A whole range of factors makes strategy implementation difficult. These include factors inside and outside the organisation. Models and frameworks are emerging to explain strategy implementation, but there is no theory of implementation that can prescribe managerial action for success. The theory and practice of implementation remains a challenge, both to managers and to researchers.

There are tools to assist managers in strategy implementation. The balanced scorecard is one such tool that is widely used in organisations to implement and monitor strategy execution. It deploys a "balanced" set of measures to evaluate strategy performance and builds required competencies and resources for more effective execution of strategies.

Porter's value chain is another tool to support strategy implementation. Porter is clear that no strategy can work without a tailor-made value chain to provide support for the strategy. The value chain is a set of activities (primary and support activities) that the organisation must perform to support any of the three generic strategies selected by the organisation. None of the three strategies will work without a reinforcing value chain. It is the value chain that determines the success or failure of strategy. The value chain, as conceived by Porter, is the whole set of managerial actions that an organisation performs and must perform to achieve the purpose and intent of its strategic option. Here Porter is talking about concrete actions, not nebulous functions.

To Mintzberg and Quinn, the problem of implementation arises because of a fundamental misconception of strategy—the separation between strategy formulation and strategy implementation. Strategic planning, as generally advocated in the strategy literature, separates strategy from implementation. Strategy is first formulated by top management. It is then implemented by the rest of the organisation. This separation is the root cause for the high rate of failure of strategy at the implementation stage. In Mintzberg's emergent strategy, strategy as patterns of action flows up from below and gets recognised and programmed as "strategies" of the organisation. Strategic planning becomes programming of strategies that already exist and are practised by managers in the organisation.

In emergent strategies, there is no separation between strategy formulation and implementation. In fact, there is no strategy formulation. There is only strategy formation. Strategies get formed throughout the organisation and get implemented by the same people. The patterns of action that emerge in organisations are generally incremental and get tested, verified, and accepted through administrative actions and routines. In this perspective, strategy formulation merges imperceptibly with strategy implementation. In this scenario, the challenges of implementation become almost irrelevant. Implementation is a challenge only when there is bifurcation between strategy formulation and strategy implementation. If strategy is decentralised patterns of action, there is less need for centralised coordination. Strategy coordination and alignment can be achieved through a system of "self-management" that Hamel propagates in his book **The Future of Management**.

Rumelt in his book **Good Strategy Bad Strategy** talks about the "kernel" of strategy as comprising three elements—diagnosis, a guiding policy, and coherent action. He argues that the actions within the kernel of strategy must be coherent. Rumelt is in favour of a more deliberate system of coordination in strategy where there is alignment between diagnosis, policy, and actions. "A strategy coordinates actions to address a specific challenge."[44] He adds: "A good strategy has coherence, coordinating actions, policies, and resources so as to accomplish an important end."[45] Strategy is about action, about doing something. But Rumelt also sees the limitation of strategic planning… "strategy is, in the language of science, a hypothesis and its implementation is an experiment."[46] A "good strategy is, in the end, a hypothesis about what will work… an educated judgement."[47] He goes further, "To generate a strategy, one must put aside the comfort and security of pure deduction and launch into the murkier waters of induction, analogy, judgement, and insight."[48] In others, both strategy formulation and implementation are a lot less rational than made out to be.

Kim and Mauborgne in blue ocean strategy attempt to integrate strategy formulation and implementation. They present eight principles of blue ocean strategy in which four principles are related to strategy execution. They are[49]:

- Overcome key organisation hurdles
- Build execution into strategy
- Align the value, profit, and people propositions
- Renew blue oceans.

The first three are particularly relevant to strategy execution. The fourth principle has more to do with sustaining strategy.

Kim and Mauborgne identify four key organisational hurdles in the way of effective strategy implementation—cognitive, limited resources, motivation, and politics. Cognitive is changing the mind-set of employees to strategic change. Leveraging limited resources is critical to effective execution. Motivating employees and other stakeholders in and outside the organisation to support strategic decisions is important. Organisational politics is the fourth organisational hurdle that needs to be overcome.

Kim and Mauborgne zero in on organisational leadership as the lever to overcome organisational hurdles—they call this "tipping point leadership." They claim "Tipping point leadership allows you to overcome these four hurdles fast and at low cost while winning employees' backing in executing a break from the status quo."[50] In other words, you need a unique kind of leadership to overcome the organisational hurdles to strategy implementation. This leadership is not based on charisma or style. It is functional—it concentrates on doing those critical things to remove obstacles to change and get the organisation working together to get things done with the limited resources it has by concentrating on "hot spots", i.e., activities that require low resources but have high impacts. Kim and Mauborgne discuss various actions that tipping point leaders can take to remove or alleviate the four organisational hurdles to strategy execution.

The second execution principle is to build execution into strategy. Here Kim and Mauborgne are talking about winning the support of all stakeholders for the strategy. Stakeholders include employees and others outside the organisation, such as suppliers and partners (external stakeholders). It is creating a "culture of trust and commitment that motivates people to execute the agreed strategy…"[51] It is winning the minds and hearts of the people beyond compulsory execution to voluntary cooperation.

To achieve this, Kim and Mauborgne introduce the concept of "fair process," which has three elements—engagement, explanation, and expectation. By engagement, they mean allowing people to participate in the strategy-making process—obtaining their inputs in strategy making. Explanation refers to communicating the final strategy arrived at so that everyone understands it and the logic behind it. Expectation refers to what is expected of everyone in the organisation in terms of implementing the strategy. People must understand clearly what is expected of them in terms of their roles, performance, and outcomes. The goals, targets, and milestones of the strategy must be clearly understood by the employees. "When people understand what is expected of them, political jockeying and favouritism are minimized, and people can focus on executing the strategy rapidly."[52] Fair process is seen as important in shaping people's attitudes and behaviour. For strategy to work, fair process must be present, both in strategy formulation and execution. Fair process applies to both internal and external stakeholders of an organisation.

The third execution principle identified by Kim and Mauborgne is aligning the value, profit, and people propositions. They state that there are three propositions essential to the success of strategy—the value proposition, the profit proposition, and the people proposition. For effective strategy formulation and implementation, there must be alignment among the three propositions. The company must create value for the customer, create profit for the company, and create benefits for the people so that they can be motivated to support and execute the strategy. "Motivating people requires more than overcoming organisational hurdles and winning people's trust with fair process. It also rests on aligned and fair incentives."[53] People here refers to both employees and external stakeholders like supply chain partners. There must be a compelling reason for external stakeholders to back the strategy. When the three strategy propositions are not properly aligned, strategy execution becomes difficult. Alignment represents a holistic understanding of strategy.

While Kim and Mauborgne do provide a framework for examining some key issues in strategy implementation, the framework does not constitute a new theory of implementation. The execution principles discussed in blue ocean strategy are not new. They are part of the existing literature on strategy implementation. They provide no new, tested prescriptions to managers on how to implement strategy. Fair process may not be enough to build execution into strategy, if strategies continue to be formulated at the top through strategic planning. Blue ocean strategy adopts a planning approach to strategy. There is separation between formulation and execution. It is top-down. There is no place for emergent strategies in blue ocean strategy. In fact, blue ocean strategy is not that different from Porter's conceptualisation of strategy. Both are rational, analytical. In such a framework, strategy implementation will continue to remain eclectic, and a challenge.

Notes

1. Ohmae [1, p. 2].
2. **Ibid**., p. 4.
3. **Ibid**., p. 4.
4. **Ibid**., p. 4.
5. **Ibid**., p. 276.
6. **Ibid**., p. 35.

7. Henkel [2, p. 4].
8. **Ibid**., p. 12.
9. **Ibid**., p. 13.
10. **Ibid**., p. 13.
11. Liedtka [3, p. 122].
12. **Ibid**., p. 122.
13. Hamel and Prahalad [4].
14. Liedtka, **op.cit**., p. 123.
15. Lawrence [5, p. 6].
16. Quoted in Lawrence, **ibid**., p. 7.
17. Mintzberg [6].
18. Quoted in Liedtka, **op.cit**., p. 123.
19. Hamel and Prahalad, quoted in Liedtka, **op.cit**., p. 123.
20. Zabriskie and Huellmantel [7].
21. Quoted in Heracleous [8, p. 482].
22. See Daft [9, pp. 413–420].
23. Rumelt [10, p. 247].
24. For an introduction to the works of these writers, the reader is advised to refer to any basic text on cross-cultural management studies.
25. Lindblom [11].
26. Quoted in Mintzberg [12, p. 108].
27. Quoted in Mintzberg, **ibid**., p. 108.
28. For a discussion of the three planning fallacies, see Mintzberg [13, p. 108].
29. For a discussion of this position, see Harari [14] and Altier [15].
30. Mintzberg [13, p. 108].
31. **Ibid**., p. 108.
32. Quoted in Henkel [16, p. 3].
33. Mintzberg [13, p. 112].
34. **Ibid**., p. 114.
35. Geus [17, p. 71].
36. Hamel [18, p. 71].
37. Ansoff [19].
38. For his ideas discussed here, see Mintzberg [12, 13, 20].
39. See Argyris [21]. Strategic planning is seen as single—loop learning.
40. Mintzberg [13, p. 108].
41. Mintzberg [20, p. 70].
42. Whittington [22].
43. Sull et al. [23].
44. Rumelt [24, p. 92].
45. **Ibid**., p. 11.
46. **Ibid**., p. 241.
47. **Ibid**., p. 243.
48. **Ibid**., p. 245.
49. Kim and Mauborgne [25, p. 23].
50. **Ibid**., p. 148.

51. **Ibid.**, p. 171.
52. **Ibid.**, p. 176.
53. **Ibid.**, p. 190.

References

1. Ohmae K (1983) The mind of the strategist. Penguin Books
2. Henkel H (2011) Can strategic thinking be taught? J Strat Leadership 3(1)
3. Liedtka J (1998) Strategic thinking: can it be taught? Long Range Plan 31(1)
4. Hamel G, Prahalad CK (1994) Competing for the future. Harvard Business School Press
5. Lawrence E (1999) Strategic thinking: a discussion paper. Prepared for the Public Service Commission of Canada, 27 Apr 1999
6. Mintzberg H (1999) Bees, flies, and CEOs. Interview with magazine Across the Board, 1 Jan 1999
7. Zabriskie NB, Huellmantel AB (1991) Developing strategic thinking in senior management. Long Range Plan 24(6)
8. Heracleous L (1998) Strategic thinking or strategic planning? Long Range Plan 31(3)
9. Daft R (2012) New era of management, 10th edn. Cengage Learning
10. Rumelt R (2013) Good strategy bad strategy. Profile Books Ltd.
11. Lindblom C (1959) The science of muddling through. Public Adm Rev 19(2)
12. Mintzberg H (1994) The rise and fall of strategic planning. Practice Hall
13. Mintzberg H (1994) The fall and rise of strategic planning. Harv Bus Rev
14. Harari O (1995) Good/bad news about strategy. Manag Rev
15. Altier W (1991) Strategic thinking for today's corporate battles. Manag Rev
16. Henkel H (2011) Can strategic thinking be taught? J Strat Leadership 3(1)
17. Geus A (1988) Planning as learning. Harv Bus Rev
18. Hamel G (1996) Strategy as revolution. Harv Bus Rev
19. Ansoff I (1965) Corporate strategy. McGraw–Hill
20. Mintzberg H (1987) Crafting strategy. Harv Bus Rev
21. Argyris C (1977 Double loop learning in organizations. Harv Bus Rev
22. Whittington R (1996) Strategy as practice. Long Range Plan 29(5)
23. Sull D, Homkes R, Sull C (2015) Why Strategy execution unravels—and what to do about it. Harv Bus Rev
24. Rumelt R (2013) Good strategy bad strategy. Profile Books
25. Kim C, Mauborgne R (2015) Blue ocean strategy. Harvard Business Review Press

Chapter 3
The I/O Model

Abstract This chapter discusses and evaluates the I/O model to strategy formulation. It essentially evaluates Porter's competitive strategy. Porter, with his emphasis on industry structure and the Five Forces, provides the best known model to strategy formulation. This chapter is a critical review of Porter's approach to strategy formulation. The strength and weakness of Porter's model are analysed. Porter is examined in the context of cross-cultural business operations and values. A significant feature of the chapter is the cross-cultural analysis of strategy, which exposes the limitations of Porter. Finally, the chapter offers a comparison with Kenichi Ohmae's strategic mind.

The chapters that follow are concerned with different conceptual models to understanding strategy. This chapter deals with the I/O model (industry organisation) to strategy formulation. The subsequent chapters discuss the other principal models found in the strategy literature. Existing strategy theory concentrates on three main areas of analysis—industry structure, company resources, and institutions. They constitute the "tripod" of strategy. The tripod of strategy, together with a new comer—blue ocean strategy,—forms the subject matter of discussion for the rest of the book.

Industry Structure

The I/O model is the industrial economics approach to strategy development. It is crafted around industry structure. Its main advocate is Michael Porter. The ideas underlying the I/O model come principally from his two books, **Competitive Strategy** (1980) and **Competitive Advantage** (1985).

To Porter, strategy is deliberate—a choice managers and firms make on how to compete in the market. He admits strategies may evolve from within the organisation (emergent strategy) but he comes on the side of explicit strategy—strategy that is deliberate, the result of planning. Managers need to formulate strategies and not wait for strategies to emerge. To compete, every firm needs a strategy–whether explicit

© The Author(s), under exclusive license to Springer Nature Singapore Pte Ltd. 2021

L. Iruthayasamy, *Understanding Business Strategy*,
https://doi.org/10.1007/978-981-33-6542-1_3

or implicit. The danger of relying on implicit strategy is that the company or firm may end up without a sustainable strategy—in other words, the firm may suffer from strategic drift. This explains why explicit strategy is important to a company. An important function of corporate management is formulating strategies that work.

To Porter, strategies are the result of analysis and planning—generally referred to as strategic planning. The starting point of strategic planning is analysis. But what do you analyse and how do you analyse? To Porter, what you need to analyse is the industry in which the firm operates or wants to enter.

Firms operate in industries. All industries are not the same. Some are more favourable to firm profitability and economic performance than others. In other words, all industries are not equally profitable. The profitability of an industry depends on how competitive it is. The less competitive, the better for the firm. This is microeconomics. In a perfect market, the firm has no bargaining power over buyers or sellers and cannot differentiate itself. It cannot set prices—it is a price taker. Such a market is obviously not conducive to a firm seeking above-average returns on its investments. The firm will not want to operate in such a market.

The ideal market for a firm in terms of profitability will be one where it has full bargaining power and control over market forces—a monopoly. In practice, the perfect and monopoly markets are the two extremes of a continuum. Firms normally operate within these two extremes where they have varying degrees of bargaining power and control. In a competitive market, if firms can establish greater control over market forces through their strategies, they stand to increase their potential for greater profitability.

The underlying idea is to reduce the power of market forces and increase firm power. All strategies—cost, differentiation, niche, or others—ultimately aim to make the firm unique and different from its competitors and thereby increase firm power. The so-called blue ocean strategy's objective is to avoid competition by operating in the blue ocean rather than in the red ocean where competition is intense. It is to compete without competing. To differentiate your products and services from those of your rivals is to increase your bargaining power and control—to move in the direction of monopolistic competition where your profit potential is higher. To reduce cost has the same objective—to have more control over market forces. In general, all strategic moves are intended to escape from free market forces and create favourable conditions where the firm can operate with less or no competition. It is to move away from the conditions of perfect competition because you do not make money under perfect competition.

Industries matter for the profitable performance of firms. It is hard to make money in some industries, like the airlines and furniture retailing. You can make more in some industries like tobacco and pharmaceuticals. Of course, there are exceptions to this. IKEA is doing well in furniture retailing. Southwest and AirAsia are doing well in the tough airline industry. But they do not disprove that market and industry structures matter. They are successful despite the adverse industry conditions because they have developed unique strategies that are exceptionally creative and imaginative. But it is harder to succeed in these markets. It is easier to succeed in industries whose competitive conditions are more favourable.

Cynthia Montgomery in her book **The Strategist** prorage profits for five industries.[1] For the period 1990–2010, the average profit for the tobacco industry was 36.1%, for pharmaceuticals 19.0%, for soft drinks 9.3%, and for airlines—10.0%. For furniture retailing for the period 2003–2010, the average profit for the industry was only 4.9%. The differences in average profits for different industries support Porter's proposition that industry matters.

How much does industry matter, really? There have been attempts to quantify the contribution of industry to firm profitability. There is no consensus on the numbers. Rumelt in a 1991 study stated that industry effects accounted for 8.0% of the variance in profitability of firms—meaning industry characteristics are not the main source of profits. The company effect on firm profitability was stated by Rumelt to be 46.0%—meaning firm characteristics are more important than industry effects on firm performance.[2] Rumelt observed, "The 'Classical' focus on industry analysis is mistaken"[3] Porter (with McGahan) in his 1997 study came to the conclusion that industry effect was greater than that stated by Rumelt—his figure was 19.0%. Porter's number for firm effect was lower—32.0 %.[4] Porter contended, "Industry proves to have a powerful direct and indirect influence on profitability".[5]

While the exact impact of industry on firm profitability remains unclear, it is accepted that industry characteristics are relevant and important to firm performance. Industries differ in their profitability. Consequently, it is important for a firm to understand the structure of the industry it is operating in because about 20% of the source of its profitability is industry related.

What explains the different profitability of industries? According to Porter, it is not just the degree of competition in the industry. Competition is just one of the forces. In his 1980 book **Competitive Strategy**, Porter identified his famous five forces as explanatory variables for industry profitability and attractiveness. The five forces are:

- Rivalry among existing competitors
- Bargaining power of buyers
- Bargaining power of suppliers
- Threat of new entrants
- Threat of substitute products or services (Fig. 3.1).

The five forces are interdependent and work as a system. It is the systemic effect of the five forces that determines how profitable an industry is or will be. The stronger the five forces, the less attractive is the industry to a firm because the potential for profit is low. If the five forces are weak, a firm operating in the industry stands to earn above-average returns on its invested capital. To perform profitably, a firm must seek to be in an attractive industry. Porter admits other factors, such as company resources, do contribute to company performance, but industry and industry structure significantly accounts for firm success. This means the structural analysis of the industry is important to firms seeking high performance. Strategy may not matter if the firm is in the wrong industry.

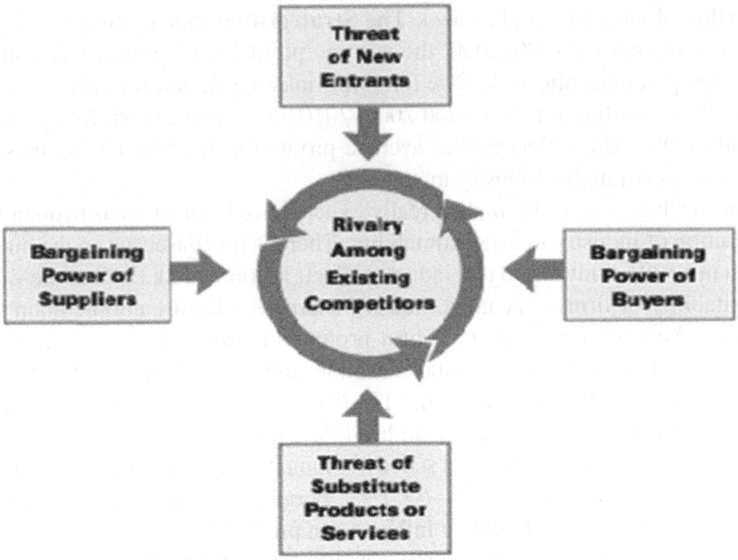

Fig. 3.1 The five forces that shape industry competition. Porter [4], p. 80

To sharpen industry analysis, Porter added an additional tool to his five forces—strategic group. Real competition in an industry takes place inside strategic groups—firms following the same or similar strategy along strategic dimensions. Identifying and mapping strategic groups in an industry can assist structural analysis.

How is industry analysis related to company strategy? How does structural analysis help firms in their strategy making? Porter answers in these words:

> Understanding the forces that shape industry competition is the starting point for developing strategy. Every company should already know what the average profitability of its industry is and how that has been changing over time. The five forces reveal why industry profitability is what it is. Only then can a company incorporate industry conditions into strategy.[6]

Porter goes on to add:

> The forces reveal the most significant aspects of the competitive environment. They also provide a baseline for sizing up a company's strengths and weaknesses: Where does the company stand versus buyers, suppliers, entrants, rivals, and substitutes? Most importantly, an understanding of industry structure guides managers toward fruitful possibilities for strategic action…[7]

Among the strategic actions Porter mentions that can flow from industry analysis are positioning the company, exploiting industry change, and shaping industry structure. Structural analysis can help a company to better cope with the current competitive forces in the industry. Porter says strategy can be viewed as "building defences against the competitive forces or finding a position in the industry where the forces are weakest."[8]

The five forces can reveal positioning opportunities in an industry that can be exploited by a firm. Industry changes and evolution provide new positioning opportunities for companies that understand the working of the competitive forces in the industry. When industry structure is in flux, new competitive opportunities emerge—like new needs or new ways of serving existing needs. Companies can also reshape industry structure—alter the five forces and lead the industry round new ways of competing. Such industry transformation is normally done by the industry leader. Industry restructuring may benefit all competitors (increase industry profit pool), but the innovator can benefit most if it can shift competition in directions where it can excel. Restructuring and improving industry can be a leader's most profitable strategic opportunity. Porter quotes the example of Sysco, the largest food-service distributor in North America, as how an industry leader can change the structure of an industry for the better. Through various strategic moves, Sysco has contributed to consolidating the industry and increasing industry profitability.[9]

The business environment has always been seen as important to company strategy, with concepts like environmental scanning, PESTEL, and SWOT. In this sense, Porter's industry analysis and the five forces are not new. What is new is the rigor that Porter brings to the analysis. Porter goes beyond generalisations about the environment and the forces in the environment that impact business policy and decision making. He zeroes in on the industry as the focal unit of analysis. Then he develops an analytical framework to analyse industry structure using five forces. Finally, he ties industry analysis to company strategy through the concept of positioning. The whole analysis is comprehensive and systemic. It is not a vague examination of the business environment and loosely tying it to company resources.

Criticism of Porter

Then, why the many criticisms against Porter? Porter takes up the major criticisms in his new Introduction to his book **Competitive Strategy** and dismisses them as misunderstandings more than challenges.[10] To be fair to Porter, many of the criticisms do reflect a lack of clear understanding of his analysis. His analysis of the industry is said to be transactional (static) when in fact Porter acknowledges that industries are dynamic and evolutionary. He points out strategic opportunities that companies can exploit in industries that are changing. He goes further and says industry leaders have a responsibility to change industries in order to raise the performance bar for all competitors so that the industry as a whole may become more profitable. In other words, Porter affirms firms operate in industries that are dynamic and companies themselves can contribute to change industry structure. The five forces are not static. They change as the industry changes and evolves, or they can be changed by industry players through their strategic moves.

Some critics argue that the five forces are inadequate to explain industry dynamics—additional factors need to be considered. In particular, they point to technology, globalisation, and government intervention as having significant impact on industry and its operations. Porter acknowledges this, but points out that they impact industry through the five forces. They only change the magnitude of the five forces. There is no need to treat them as separate or additional forces for purposes of analysing industry structure. There is no need for a sixth force.[11]

Then there is the problem of industry boundaries. Where does an industry begin and where does it end? Rigorous industry analysis is not possible if boundaries are shifting all the time. Porter recognises this and says, "Defining the industry in which competition actually takes place is important for good industry analysis... Many strategy errors emanate from mistaking the relevant industry, defining it too broadly or too narrowly."[12] Then Porter proceeds to discuss two dimensions of industry boundaries—product scope and geographic scope. He posits that the five forces can help analyse the two dimensions and clarify the boundary issues in industry.

Despite what Porter says, the boundary issue is a serious challenge. His analytical framework is ideal for a closed system. As the system opens up with global operations and increased linkages with partners and even competitors, industry boundaries become blurred. As new linkages and partnerships get established and as competition cuts across industries and companies operate in diverse industries, identifying industry boundaries becomes a real challenge. Porter's five forces may help sort out some of these complexities, but it is an area that needs more study. The five forces may be able to handle industry changes and dynamics, but their capacity as a tool for analysing overlapping industries is open to debate.

But the real problem with Porter's industry analysis lies elsewhere. There is little doubt about its importance to strategy. Companies compete in industries. Industries are important because they account for about 20% of company profitability. To compete successfully, companies need to understand the competitive environment in the industry and what accounts for the degree of competition in it. It is here that the five forces are useful. The five forces are tools for analysing the competition in an industry. Based on the industry analysis, firms can plan and formulate appropriate strategies to compete in the industry. Understanding the industry is also important because industries vary in their profitability. Some industries are more profitable than others. The profitability of an industry is determined by the degree of competition in the industry—that is, by the strength of the five forces. Firms would naturally want to operate in a profitable industry or, if they are in a declining industry, they would need to influence the five forces to create a more favourable competitive environment for themselves. They would do this through planned strategic actions.

It does not matter what is the nature of the industry or where it is located. The need for structural analysis is there—it is the precondition for strategic planning and strategy formulation. It applies to all industries—emerging, mature, declining, fragmented, and global. The competitive environment in each industry calls for different strategic moves. Without structural analysis to understand the competitive environment of an industry, it would not be possible for a company to develop the right strategies to compete.

The problem is not with the need for structural analysis. Structural analysis is necessary for strategy formulation. The problem is: How does corporate management do it? How do mangers in companies go about doing structural analysis using Porter's five forces? Porter does provide some guidelines in his book **Competitive Strategy** on how to do structural analysis. In particular, he has a chapter in the book on "A Framework for Competitor Analysis" and an Appendix B "How to Conduct an Industry Analysis." Porter cannot be faulted for not providing enough information on it. The problem is not lack of information on how to do industry analysis but too much information on how to do it. This comes from Porter's attempt to be comprehensive and systemic in his approach to industry analysis. He confirms it himself in his book on competitive strategy when he says "This book presents a comprehensive framework of analytical techniques to help a firm analyse its industry as a whole and predict the industry's future evolution, to understand its competitors and its own position, and to translate this analysis into a competitive strategy for a particular business."[13]

Whilst this may be good for the theory of industry analysis, it ignores the reality of managerial thinking and behaviour. Porter says the book is written for "practitioners, that is, managers seeking to improve the performance of their businesses..."[14] Porter is prescriptive in his approach to industry analysis and strategy formulation. He is telling managers how to do analysis and formulate strategies. If Porter is to be relevant to managers, his prescription must fall within the ambit of managerial thinking, behaviour, and decision making. This does not appear to be the case.

Porter's entire approach to industry analysis and strategy formulation is based on the assumption that the typical manager is highly rational and analytical in his thinking and behaviour. This does not square with the work of many leading managerial and organisational theorists. Mintzberg's research on the nature of managerial work presents a different description of how managers actually work and take decisions. Managers are more reactive than proactive, decision processes are disorderly and political, and most planning is informal and adaptive.[15] If this the true nature of managerial work, Porter's rational, comprehensive, and systemic foundation for strategic analysis and planning cannot be an operational guide to the manager. Managers do not go about analysing and making strategic decisions the way Porter advocates. Porter's model then becomes merely prescriptive. It is not descriptive of how managers actually do analysis and develop strategies.

This is apparent from the informational and analytical demand that Porter's structural analysis places on the corporate manager. Porter's analysis simply demands too much information and analytical capability from the busy manager. Information is needed not only about the present but, more importantly, about the future. Porter stresses the importance of understanding market signals. "Recognising and accurately reading market signals… is of major significance for developing competitive strategy…".[16]

If markets and industries are dynamic, changing, and evolving, if competition is not only for the present but for the future, how does the manager deal with the information demands of the present and the future? How does he predict the future? Porter holds the view that industries are largely stable and the manager is not required to make "heroic predictions" of the future. This is open to debate. The pace of industry evolution is different today, mainly because of disruptive technologies. It is expected that the Fourth Wave of industrialization will be more invasive than the first three. It will fundamentally change the way we live and work. This in turn will change how business is done. All this will impact industry structure. The effect will be substantial, not tangential. Future industries may not be the same as present industries. One may need new analytical tools to examine industries. Porter's contention that true disruptive technologies are rare may not be well founded. Porter is right in claiming that technology changes generally affect industry structure through altering the five forces. But major technology changes destroy existing industries and create new ones. They fundamentally alter customer needs and how these needs are met. They change how business is done—they have a revolutionary effect on industry structure. To treat their effects tangentially, as Porter does, may not do justice to the importance of technology in strategy development.

Even if Porter is right about industry stability, the information and analytical demand made by his five forces is beyond most managers. Porter's assumption of rationality for managerial action is shaky. Herbert Simon in 1947 had pointed out that administrative behaviour is not rational—at best it can be described as only "bounded rationality".[17] Lindblom had said that administrators "muddle through" in their decision making.[18] Quinn describes the manager's analytical process as "logical incrementalism".[19] Other organisational theorists like Cyert and March had also questioned rationality in organisations.[20] The limitations on rational administrative behaviour had led Simon to advocate "satisficing" as an alternative to full rationality. The manager only satisfices—he does not optimise. He looks for "good enough" decisions, not the "best". The manager is an "administrative man" not an "economic man". Quinn advocates a similar approach—incremental analysis to problem solving.

The work of organisational theorists does not support the rational-comprehensive approach to analysis advocated by Porter. It is just beyond the capability of managers and the many organisational constraints under which they work. This is especially the case if industry analysis and strategic planning are left in the hands of a small group of people at the top (strategic planning unit), with little involvement of line managers lower down the organisation. In such cases, strategic analysis and planning can become divorced from the realities of organisational life. To be relevant and meaningful to managers, strategic analysis and strategic planning must be rooted in the realities of managerial work.

The question of rationality goes beyond organisations. It needs to be understood in the context of countries and national cultures. Rational thinking and behaviour is not the same everywhere. What is rational in one country may not be rational in another. Even in the West, American rationality is not necessarily the same as French or German rationality. This explains why American, French, and Germans take different policy decisions with respect to international issues. The facts may be the same, but their analysis and understanding is different and therefore the policy choices made are different.

There is enough evidence to support the thesis that Asian thinking and rationality is different from that of the West. If organizational rationality is limited and if rationality varies with country and national culture, there may be a need to revisit Porter's five forces as they rest on a fundamental assumption that firms operating in an industry act and behave rationally—that is, on Western concepts of rationality.[21]

The five forces rest on the values of a free enterprise system (capitalism), with profit as the primary goal of business. In a society based on a different socio-economic-political philosophy, Porter's five forces may not have the same relevance. Porter's industry analysis is based on competition. In the West, competition is seen not only as a tool to win but as a value in itself. Competition is good and desirable. This is not a universal perspective. In many societies, especially in Asia, cooperation is a more important value than competition.

In Japanese, Chinese, and Korean companies with strong foundations in Confucian values and traditions, the desire to cooperate, even with your competitors, is strong. Harmony is an important value, not confrontation. This does not mean Japanese, Chinese, and Korean companies do not compete. They compete fiercely, both locally and globally. But their attitude to competition and cooperation/collaboration is different. Profit, while important, is not an overriding business goal. Relationships are important. All partners up and down the supply and value chain must benefit.

The Confucian concept of family obligations and ethical behaviour is extended to business operations. Business is not a single unit but a "family". You do business with your family and clan. The structure and operations of overseas Chinese companies in South and East Asia clearly demonstrate the family and social ties that bind these companies together. The goal is not profit maximization for any one particular company in the group. In fact, profit opportunities maybe sacrificed for the larger good of the family and clan.

The system works on collaboration and filial obligations. Of course there is competition between rival families, but this is different from the kind of competition that Porter is talking about. The family clusters of the overseas Chinese business are different from the strategic groups of Porter. In Porter's strategic groups, there is intense competition. In the family and clan structure of the overseas Chinese and other Asian groups, there is more collaboration and social obligations to each other. The overseas Chinese method of doing business in Asia does not quite fit with Porter's competitive rationality. This does not mean companies in the West do not collaborate with other companies. They do, but it is not comparable to the overseas Chinese business structure and operations.

Given the difficulties associated with Porter's industry analysis, is there a less demanding way to look at industries and understand the underlying forces for success in them? Kenichi Ohmae provides one helpful tool—KFS or key factors for success.[22] The premise is that every industry has a small number of critical factors that determines the success or failure of firms in the industry. There are many forces at work in an industry, but only a few matter in terms of how a firm should compete in the industry. Firms in the industry that do not meet the requirements of the critical factors are unlikely to succeed. The KFS can be said to represent the secret of success in the industry. Ohmae quotes an example—the lumber industry. The lumber industry has only two KFS—owning large forests and maximizing the yield from them. Once the KFS has been identified, the company can then proceed to explore the details related to the KFS—for example, how to maximise the yield from the forests. The company probes in depth how the critical factors impact business operations in the industry. Ohmae believes there is no need for perfect information. The strategist must avoid a "perfectionist obsession with details". There is no "perfect strategy". What is vital in strategy is timing. Ohmae adds:

> The key to victory… lies in developing a market strategy that will give you an edge – even a slight edge – on the competition and then putting it into effect at exactly the right moment.[23]

The KFS approach allows the manager to free himself from perfectionism and focus on those few critical factors that determine success in the industry. Ohmae quotes examples of KFS in different industries. For example, in shipbuilding and steelmaking, it is economies of scale in manufacturing. In the beer industry, it is economies of scale but in distribution, not manufacturing. In ice cream, it is seasonal variation and refrigeration.

How does one identify the KFS of an industry? Through talking to experts in the industry and market research. The initial identification may only be a hypothesis, which is then probed, amended, and verified through empirical work. This is how most consultants go about looking at industries and making strategy recommendations to companies.

KFS is not without problems. It tends to be transactional. It looks at critical success factors at a point of time. But what determines success today may not determine success tomorrow. Industries evolve and therefore the success factors can be totally different for the future. Companies need to develop strategies not only for the present but also for the future. As Hamel and Prahalad emphasize, real strategy is about competing for the future. To develop strategies for the future, which is evolving all the time, requires forecasting KFS for future industries. This is a great challenge. The greatest strength of the KFS perspective to industry analysis is that it simplifies the analytical process for managers. It removes much of the complexity found in the Porter framework. The KFS perspective makes it possible for companies to allocate their scarce resources to those critical factors in the industry that will make a difference. Knowing the KFS of an industry does not mean all firms in the industry will adopt the same strategy to compete. Various strategy options are still open to different competitors, including changing the KFS of the industry, which is changing the rules of the game. The job of the manager is to achieve superior relative performance (relative to the competitor) in the key factors for success of the business.

Porter, of course, does not think KFS can explain industry and how it operates. You need a systemic understanding of the fundamentals to analyse industry and its operations, which he believes only his framework provides.

The prescriptive model of Porter also suffers from the "one-best-way" syndrome. In this regard, it is similar to Taylor's one-best-way to manage. Porter believes his five forces can analyse any industry in any location. There is no need to look at other variables to explain the workings of an industry. All industries, including new industries, are conditioned by the five forces. Other variables that can impact industry, like government intervention and technology, operate through the five forces. They are not independent forces influencing industry structure and operations.

Is the on-best-way perspective realistic, or are there other ways of looking at competition? What are the assumptions behind Porter's industry analysis? Porter's five forces rest on three important assumptions:

- The industry is operating under free market conditions
- Competition is good
- The primary goal of business is profit.

These assumptions are not necessarily true in all countries. In most countries, governments intervene to influence market forces. The intervention is less where the free enterprise system is strong, like in the United State. In communist countries, like North Korea, the intervention is absolute. Here, the five forces are replaced by centralised planning. In many emerging countries, government intervention is substantial. It is not an appendix to the five forces, as Porter would like us to believe. Governments establish and manage enterprises that are protected by legislations, tariffs, and subsidies. These state enterprises, like in China, form an important component of the industry structure. The five forces are not relevant to the state enterprises. They operate on a different basis.

Apart from direct participation, governments in emerging countries impact industry structure and competition in numerous ways—legislations, subsidies, licensing, policies, affirmative actions, and many more when government intervention reaches a certain level, the economy is no longer "free"—it is "administered." What determines the structure of industry and its competitive environment then is not the five forces but government. When intervention reaches this level, "government" may well be considered the sixth force in Porter's taxonomy. If you look at many of the so-called "entrepreneurs" in these countries, they are not the typical Silicon Valley type—someone who had a novel business idea, started in a garage or university dorm, and grew the business through creativity and innovation. The typical entrepreneur in emerging countries is likely to be one who built his success through connections with the government of the day. It is government support, protection, and favoured treatment that would explain his success, not Porter's five forces or the competitive strategies derived from them. One has to be cautious in generalising Porter's framework.

The assumption of "competition" in Porter's model was discussed earlier. "Competition is good" is essentially a Western value. There are other perceptions of competition. In general, Asians place emphasis on cooperation and collaboration, not competition. This comes from Asian culture—the importance of harmony, family, and filial obligations. The general approach to business strategy developed by Porter and others from the West is competition based. If competition is not valued in a society or valued less, competition-based strategies will apply less to such societies. Competition is not a universal value.

Similarly with profit. Porter is clear on the purpose of strategy. It is to earn superior returns on invested capital. Strategies are formulated to create competitive advantage. Through competitive advantage, firms hope to maximize profits. Strategy and profits are linked. What if the emphasis is not on maximizing profits but on some other values? Profits maybe traded off for other outcomes. The role of filial obligation under Confucianism was discussed earlier and how overseas Chinese companies assist clan members in business. Clearly, these companies do not consider profit to be their only or primary goal.

The key question is: What is the purpose of business? If the purpose is more than profit and includes an obligation to society and the community, it means making some trade-offs between profit and its other obligations. The whole CSR movement is part of this argument. If profit is only one of the goals of a company, how do the concepts and principles of strategic analysis and strategy formulation apply? These concepts and principles aim to maximize profits, not trade-off profit opportunities to meet social obligations. The pressure on business to be socially responsible is growing everywhere. Wall Street is under attack. Strategy frameworks need to give more specific thought and space to the social side of business. The foundations of strategic analysis may have to shift from profit to a blending of profit and social obligations—to something similar to Confucian companies.

A good example that demonstrates the limitation of existing strategy frameworks is Islamic management. In Porter's model, the ultimate test of a successful strategy is financial returns—specifically, the rate of return on invested capital. But in Islamic management, what is more important is whether the company has complied with "Syariah" principles and tenets. Profits are necessary, but they must be earned in a "halal" way. The company will be judged on whether it has been Islamic in its operations—not so much on how much money it has made. The strategy prescriptions that Porter provides are of limited help to Islamic companies operating on economic and social foundations that are different from the West. Islamic banking, Islamic insurance, and Islamic investment all need different analytical and strategy tools that are consistent with Islamic perspectives of business.

Kenichi Ohmae's Strategic Triangle

Finally, Porter's structural analysis is not the only model for understanding industries. Kenichi Ohmae provides an alternative model—the strategic triangle. He says "In the construction of any business strategy, three main players must be taken into account: the corporation itself, the customer, and the competition."[24] These are the three C's of strategic analysis. A successful strategy is one that better matches corporate strength to customer needs than the competitor. Ohmae defines strategy "as the way in which a corporation endeavours to differentiate itself positively from its competitors, using its relative corporate strengths to better satisfy customer needs."[25] It follows that strategies should be developed based on the strategic triangle—that is, customer-based strategies, corporate-based strategies, and competitor-based strategies (Fig. 3.2).

Ohmae emphasizes that customer-based strategies are the basis of all strategies. Companies must follow the changing needs of customers. The basic mission of business is to serve its customers more effectively than its competitors. As Drucker said, the purpose of business is to create a customer.

Corporate-based strategy is functional—to maximize the strength of the corporation relative to the competition. Its role depends on the nature of the business and the KFS of the industry. Here Ohmae is talking about a corporation in a single business,

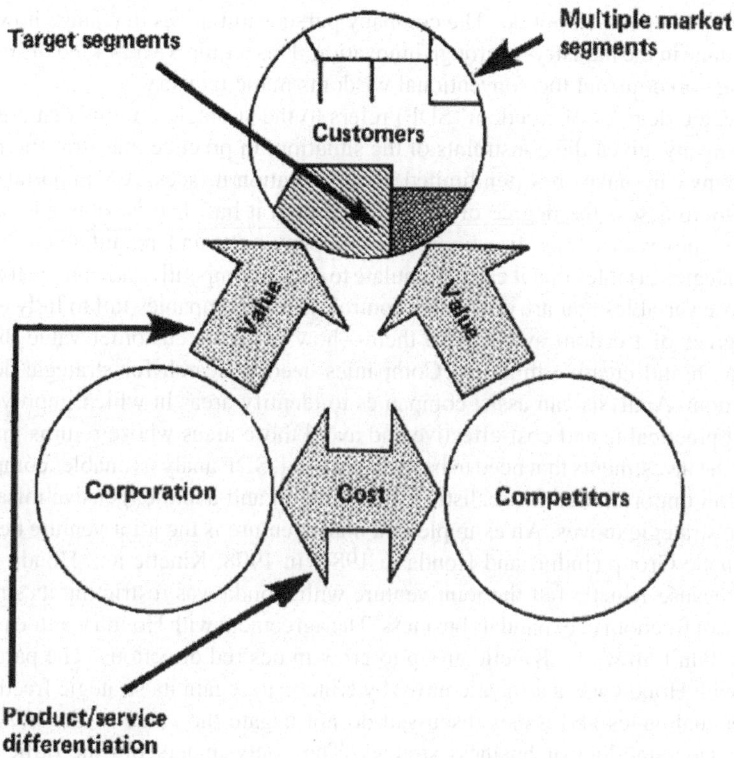

Fig. 3.2 The strategic three C's *Source* Ohmae [14], p. 92

not a conglomerate with many distinct businesses. He is not talking about corporate strategy in the context of a diversified company.

Competitor-based strategies are designed to create differentiation from competitors. Ohmae stresses that "any differences between you and your competitors must be related to one or more of the three elements that jointly determine profit: price, volume, and cost."[26]

Ohmae suggests four routes to creating competitive advantage: (1) KFS analysis, (2) relative superiority, (3) aggressive initiatives, and (4) strategic degrees of freedom. KFS has been discussed earlier. The other three routes to strategic advantage as proposed by Ohmae are described below.[27]

To Ohmae, absolute superiority is not necessary. What is important is to establish relative superiority—relative to what the competitor is offering. One way to do this is to compare your product with your competitor's—analysing the differences and determining how you can achieve relative advantage in price, cost, or quality. Relative superiority can be established in many areas—product, operations, and services.

In aggressive initiatives, the company attempts to change the KFS of an industry—change the rules of the game. The company realises operational improvements or doing more better will not do. The company pursues initiatives to change how business is done in the industry—through innovation. This requires a new kind of strategic thinking—to confront the conventional wisdoms in the industry.

Strategic degrees of freedom (SDF) refers to the strategic options that are open to a company, given the constraints of the situation. In practice, the strategic moves a company can make are often limited by the situation it faces. It is important for a company to assess the degree of strategic freedom it has, if it is to avoid wasteful strategic moves in wrong directions. The company must understand and assess the key strategic variables that it can manipulate to create competitive advantage for itself and those variables that are outside its control. Often, companies fail to fully exploit the degrees of freedom available to them—how to create customer value through innovation and creative thinking. Companies need to search for strategic degrees of freedom. Analysis can assist companies to identify areas in which improvement is most practicable and cost-effective and avoid those areas whose returns may not justify the investments that need to be made. In brief, SDF analysis enables companies to exploit opportunities for realistic differentiation and avoid expensive misadventures in strategic moves. An example of a misadventure is the joint venture between the Kinetic Group (India) and Honda in 1984. In 1998, Kinetic and Honda parted ways because Kinetic felt the joint venture with Honda was restricting its strategic degrees of freedom to expand its business. The agreement with Honda was too restrictive. It didn't allow the Kinetic group to grow in desired directions. The parting of ways with Honda was a strategic move by Kinetic to regain its strategic freedom.

The challenges and issues discussed do not negate the value of the I/O model to our understanding of business strategy. They only underscore the difficulty of prescribing any specific strategy for business success.

Notes

1. Montgomery [1], p. 48.
2. Rumelt [2], p. 168.
3. Rumelt **ibid.**, p. 168.
4. McGahan and Porter [3], p. 23.
5. **Ibid.**, p.16.
6. Porter [4], p. 88.
7. **Ibid.**, p 88.
8. **Ibid.**, p. 89.
9. **Ibid.**, p. 90.
10. Porter [5].
11. **Ibid.**, p. xv.
12. Porter [4], p. 91.
13. Porter [5], p. xxii.
14. **Ibid.** p. xxiii.
15. See Yukl [6], pp. 76–102.
16. Porter [7], p. 75.
17. Simon [8].

18. Lindblom [9].
19. James Quinn said the following about the planning process in his 1980 book:

    > My date suggest that when well-managed major organizations make significant changes in strategy, the approaches they use frequently bear little resemblance to the rational, analytical systems so often described in the planning literature.

    Quoted in Mintzberg [10], p. 108.
20. See Cyert and March [11].
21. For a discussion of different modes of thinking and the impact of national cultures and values on decision making, see [12], pp. 63–86. Also see [13], pp. 42–63.
22. Ohmae [14].
23. **Ibid.**, p. 80.
24. **Ibid.**, p. 91.
25. **Ibid.**, p. 92.
26. **Ibid.**, p. 126.
27. **Ibid.**, p. 38.

References

1. Montgomery C (2012) The strategist. Harper Collins Publishers
2. Rumelt R (1991) How much does industry matter? Strateg Manage J 12(3)
3. McGahan A, Porter M (1997) How much does industry matter, really? Strateg Manage J 18(Summer Special Issue)
4. Porter M (2008) The five competitive forces that shape strategy. Harv Bus Rev
5. Porter M (1980) Competitive strategy, introduction 1998. The Free Press
6. Yukl G (2010) Leadership in organizations. Pearson
7. Porter M (1980) Competitive strategy. The Free Press
8. Simon H (1947) Administrative behavior. The Free Press
9. Lindblom C (1959) The science of muddling through. Publ Adm Rev 19(2)
10. Mintzberg H (1994) The rise and fall of strategic planning. Prentice Hall
11. Cyert R, March J (1963) A behavioral theory of the firm. Prentice Hall
12. Lourdesamy I (2017) Management: universal or culture bound. In: New frontiers of management. Cengage Learning Asia
13. Hofstede G (1980) Motivation, leadership and organization: do American theories apply abroad? Organ Dyn Summer
14. Ohmae K (1982) The mind of the strategist. Penguin Books

Chapter 4
The Resource-Based View

Abstract The Resource-Based View (RBV) as a major alternative to the I/O model in business strategy is the focus of this chapter. The question whether industry or firm resources matter in formulating strategy is the key issue in the discussions. Firm resources in their complexity are identified and explained in terms of their contribution to strategy formulation. Included is the concept of sustainable competitive advantage and the unique resources a firm must possess (VRIO) in order to have sustainable competitive advantage. The concept of 'core competence' within the RBV model is discussed. A variance—organisational capabilities—is also taken up. Prahalad and Hamel conceive a corporation as a collection of unique competencies, not products or business units. Competitive advantage is to be achieved based on their core competence. This notion is clearly different from Porter's industry analysis in strategy formulation. Does this mean RBV constitutes a new theory of strategy? This question guides the discussions in this chapter.

What is the relationship between company resources and strategy? How do firm resources influence strategy formulation?

The strategy literature acknowledges that firm performance is largely determined by the industry in which the firm operates and the attributes of the firm. The exact impact of industry and firm on performance remains contentious. Rothaermel states that industry accounts for about 20% of firm performance, while firm effects explain between 30 and 45% of its performance.[1] Clearly, firms and what they do appear to be a major determinant of business success. This is despite the preoccupation of Porter with industry analysis.

What exactly in the firm explains business performance and success? The resource-based view of the firm (RBV) attempts to provide the answer—it is the unique bundle of resources and capabilities possessed by the firm. The RBV perspective of business strategy emerged in the 1980s, partly as a reaction to Ansoff's rational planning and Porter's positioning approaches to strategy formulation. The resource-based theory to strategy can be traced back to Wernerfelt's 1984 article "A Resource-Based View of the Firm."[2] The perspective gained real attention in 1990 with Prahalad and Hamel's HBR article "The Core Competence of the Corporation".[3] But, as a theory of competition, RBV took shape only in 1991 with Barney's article

© The Author(s), under exclusive license to Springer Nature Singapore Pte Ltd. 2021

L. Iruthayasamy, *Understanding Business Strategy*,
https://doi.org/10.1007/978-981-33-6542-1_4

"Firm Resources and Sustained Competitive Advantage."[4] In this article, Barney laid out the details of the RBV framework as a theory of competitive advantage—how firms can achieve sustainable competitive advantage by possessing, developing, or acquiring "organizational resources that are valuable, rare, difficult to imitate and non-substitutable."[5]

The RBV presents a different understanding of strategic analysis from Ansoff's strategic planning or Porter's industry analysis. In the Porter's model, the unit of analysis is the industry. In Barney's RBV, the unit of analysis is firm resources. Porter's emphasis is external—the industry and its structure. Barney's focus is internal—the firm and its resources. For Porter, it is the industry that determines firm performance. For Barney, it is what resources a firm has that determine its success and sustainability.

Firm Resources

A resource is anything that can be thought of as strength of the firm. It includes both tangible and intangible assets. The RBV literature has identified six categories of resources: financial resources, physical resources, human resources, technical resources, reputation, and organisational resources. Resources are inputs that go into or assist the production process.

A unique resource of the firm that is different from other resources is capabilities. Resources themselves do not produce value. They have to be deployed, coordinated, and exploited in a cost-effective manner to produce value for customers. This requires special capabilities or competencies. Generally, capabilities are firm-specific. They are part of organisational culture and are difficult to be imitated by competitors. For this reason, capabilities are treated as the main source of a firm's competitive advantage.

Conceptually, RBV has been evolving since first mooted by Penrose and Wernerfelt.[6] But its basic tenets have remained, which are:

- Firms have a bundle of resources and capabilities.
- Firm resources are heterogeneous. That is, firms vary in their resources and capabilities.
- Firm resources are generally immobile, that is, the resources cannot be transferred from firm to firm without cost. Firm resources are "sticky."
- Valuable firm resources are a source of competitive advantage for the firm. Valuable resources controlled by a firm enable the firm to conceive and implement value-creating strategies.
- Competitive advantage cannot exist for firms with identical resources and capabilities. If firms possess exactly the same resources (same amount and kind), no firm can conceive and implement a differential strategy.

The above concepts provide the foundation for the RBV theory of competition based on firm resources. But not all firm resources are a source of competitive advantage. A firm can have many kinds of resource, as identified earlier. But not all of them may be valuable in terms of contributing to competitive advantage. In the RBV literature, resources are valuable "when they enable a firm to conceive of or implement strategies that improve its efficiency and effectiveness"[7] and "when they exploit opportunities or neutralise threats in a firm's environment."[8] In other words, they must contribute to creating competitive advantage. Competitive advantage is defined as "implementing a value-creating strategy not simultaneously being implemented by any current or potential competitors."[9]

In the RBV perspective, valuable resources a firm possesses or controls provide the foundation for developing strategies to compete in the market. In other words, firm profitability comes from resources. In the Porter's model, a firm's ability to earn economic rent depends on the industry structure. In RBV, it is firm resources and capabilities that provide the direction for firm strategy and the source of its profit.

Robert Grant provides a framework for a resource-based approach to strategy formulation. The framework is a five-stage process for strategy analysis and strategy formulation—analysing the firm's resources; appraising the firm's capabilities; analysing the profit-earning potential of the firm's resources and capabilities; selecting a strategy; and extending and upgrading the firm's pool of resources and capabilities (Fig. 4.1).

But the competitive advantage provided by valuable firm resources can be temporary. The resources may not be unique, though valuable. If the resources can be imitated or replicated by competitors, the competitive advantage enjoyed by the firm can be eroded. It will not sustain. To sustain competitive advantage, the firm strategy must be based on resources that are unique and firm-specific—resources that competitors cannot easily acquire or develop on their own.

What are these unique firm resources that can sustain competitive advantage? Barney has developed what is referred to as the VRIO test for sustainability. For a firm to develop sustainable competitive advantage, its resources must be[10]:

- Valuable
- Rare
- Difficult to imitate
- Non-substitutable

Barney defines sustainable competitive advantage differently from Porter. Generally, sustainability is defined as a competitive advantage that persists over time. But to Barney "competitive advantage is sustained only if it continues to exist after efforts to duplicate that advantage have ceased."[11]

In one sense, RBV is not new. It is only an extension of SWOT. It matches the strengths and weaknesses of the firm with the opportunities and threats in the market. It is concerned with "strategic fit" between the firm and its environment. It brings internal and external analysis together. But RBV takes the conceptual model of SWOT to a higher analytical level by linking firm resources to competitive advantage and strategy. Whether this constitutes a theory of competition is another matter, which will be discussed later.

RBV is not one unified theory of the firm. Within it, there are different strains of thinking. The unit of analysis is the same—the firm and its resources. Competitive advantage and profitability are seen as deriving from firm resources, not industry. This is a fundamental departure from Porter and his industry analysis. But within the RBV framework, there are variations in thinking and analysis. Which firm resources

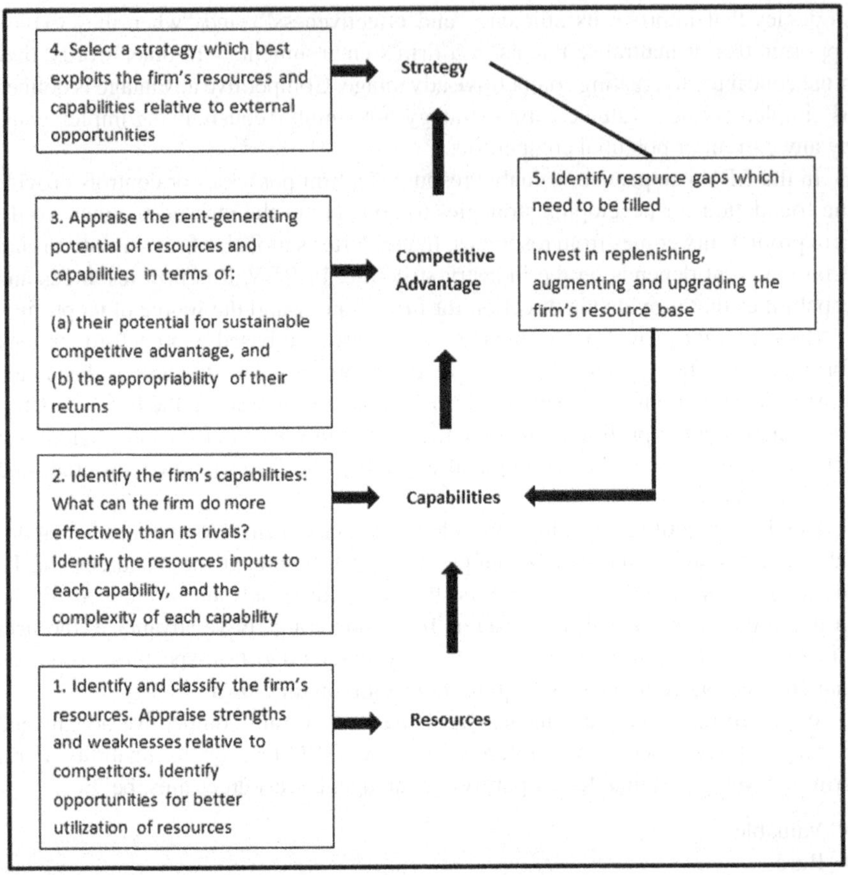

Fig. 4.1 A resource-based approach to strategy analysis: a practical framework. *Source* Grant [1, p. 115]

are more critical? Which resources really sustain competitive advantage? How are firm resources linked to business strategy? How should firm resource be analysed—in terms of economics or other disciplines, like sociology and organisation theory? Given this diversity of perspectives, there is no one RBV but several RBVs.

In terms of orientation, both RBV and Porter's industry analysis are economic-based approaches. Porter argues that competitive advantage is determined by economic forces in the industry—specifically, his five forces. His framework is built on the structure-conduct-performance (SCP) paradigm of industrial organisation economics. The essence of the paradigm is that firm performance in the market depends on the characteristics of the industry in which it operates. Profit is found not in the firm but in the structure of the industry, specifically in the nature of the five forces. To Porter, strategy is about taking offensive and defensive actions to cope with the five forces. He concedes that firms can formulate strategies to achieve superior economic performance by changing industry structure and the rules of competition, but, essentially, firm performance depends on selecting the right industry and correct positioning.

In both RBV and Porter's approach, the objective of business strategy is maximization of rents, but the nature of rents is different. Porter's approach is built around market power and monopoly rent. To Porter, competitive advantage comes from impeding competitive forces that can drive economic returns down by creating entry mobility barriers. The idea is to retain market power and blunt competition. RBV is an efficiency-based explanation of differences in firm performance. Superior resources are more efficient in that they enable a firm to produce more economically or satisfy customer wants better. RBV is concerned with Ricardian rents derived from scarcity of superior resources.

Robert Grant argues that "business strategy should be viewed less as a quest for monopoly rents (the returns to market power) and more as a quest for Ricardian rents (the return to the resources which confer competitive advantage over and above the real costs of these resources)."[12] When these resources depreciate, become obsolete, or are replicated by competitors, the rents they generate tend to disappear. In other words, Grant believes business strategy should rest on resources rather than on monopoly power. He further posits that industry analysis cannot be divorced from resources. "A closer look at market power and the monopoly rent it offers suggests that it too has its basis in the resources of firms."[13] Market power depends on the presence of barriers to entry. "Barriers to entry are based upon scale economies, patents, experience advantages, brand reputation, or some other resource which incumbent firms possess but which entrants can acquire only slowly or at disproportionate expense."[14] It is resources that confer market power on firms. In other words, industry analysis for strategy formulation cannot be separated from RBV. Flore Bridoux emphasises the same point when she says "returns from entering and operating in an industry cannot be evaluated independently of the firm's resources and capabilities."[15] But Porter is emphatic in his view on resources. He stresses, "Resources are not valuable in and of themselves, but because they allow firms to perform activities that create advantages in particular markets."[16]

What is Porter really saying? He is not dismissing resources, but sees them in a supportive role. In Porter's theory of competition, there are three elements: industry analysis, positioning, and value chain. The three elements fit together and function as a system. Strategy and competitive advantage involve all three elements. Value chain activities are critically important for sustaining competitive advantage. A strategy, no matter how robust or good, cannot be sustained without the firm performing a set of activities to support the strategy. This applies to both cost and differentiation strategies. Cost strategies require a different set of activities from differentiation strategies. To carry out these activities effectively, the firm requires different resources—information, skills, competencies, systems, processes, networks, etc. Different resources are needed for different market situations and strategy choices. Resources support the value chain activities that need to be performed. In other words, Porter sees resources as a complement to the I/O model of strategy formulation and implementation.

Firm resources are relevant to strategy implementation—to support firm activities that are needed to execute the firm's chosen strategy. The relevance and value of firm resources is determined by the positioning the firm has chosen. If the positioning of the firm should change (repositioning) as a consequence of structural changes in the industry or for other reasons, the relevance and value of firm resources will also change. Some of the old resources of the firm may become obsolete. New resources may be required to support a new set of value chain activities of the firm. Seen in this context, firm resources have no independent value of their own—they are only inputs to help firms formulate and execute their strategies and sustain competitive advantage. Given Porter's perspective of RBV, does the resource approach make any contribution to the understanding of business strategy?

The point was raised in 2001 by Priem and Butler in their article "Is the Resource-Based "View" A Useful Perspective For Strategic Management Research?"[17] They levelled several criticisms at RBV as expounded by Barney in his 1991 article "Firm Resources and Sustained Competitive Advantage."[18] Their three major areas of criticism were: (1) it is the market that determines the value of each firm resource; (2) the methodology presented for determining the value of firm resources was tautological; and (3) RBV, as a theory of competitive advantage, did not meet the test of theory. These criticisms of RBV still stand today, although Barney and others have made attempts to refute them.[19]

Does this mean RBV has nothing to contribute to business strategy? Not so. Porter himself has acknowledged the relevance of firm resources to positioning and performance of value chain activities. RBV is particularly relevant where the business environment is changing only incrementally, which means firm resources are more stable. The resource view is also valuable in assessing opportunities for business diversification. Empirical studies clearly show that firm attributes contribute more significantly to firm profitability than industry. In other words, firms do matter—which means firm resources and capabilities make a difference to the economic performance of companies.

Core Competence

The question is not whether resources matter. They do. The real question is: Is RBV an alternative theory of strategy?—that is, alternative to industry analysis. If there is any strand within RBV that has potential to develop into a theory of competition, it would be the "core competence" view of the firm presented by Prahalad and Hamel. The idea that a corporation is a collection of competencies and not products and businesses was first mooted by Prahalad and Hamel in a HBR article called "The Core Competence of the Corporation."[20] The RBV was initially concerned with firm "resources." Over time, attention shifted to new resources, such as "capabilities", "core competence," and "dynamic capabilities." Whether there is any real difference between them is debatable. Barney expresses the point in these words:

> Although these distinctions among resources, capabilities, and competencies can be drawn in theory, it is likely they will become badly blurred in practice. In particular, it seems

unlikely that a debate whether a particular firm attributes is a "resource" and "capability" or a "competence" will be of much value to managers or firms.[21]

But Barney does concede "core competence" may have special implications for firm diversification. Prahalad and Hamel believe the core competence of a firm is different from its other resources. They see a firm as a portfolio of different competencies, not products or business units. Here they are talking about a diversified company. To them, how managers conceive the corporation is important. If they conceive the corporation in terms of price/performance attributes of current products, the strategies they pursue will be different—it will be short-term strategising. But if managers perceive their corporation as a collection of unique competencies that their competitors do not possess, their strategies will be different. They will compete for competitive advantage based on their core competence.

What specifically is a core-competence? Prahalad and Hamel provide an analogy. "The diversified corporation is a large tree. The trunk and major limbs are core products, the smaller branches are business units; the leaves, flowers, and fruit are end products. The root system that provides nourishment, sustenance, and stability is the core competence."[22] They stress that "core competencies are the collective learning in the organization, especially how to coordinate diverse production skills and integrate multiple streams of technologies."[23] Core competence requires communication and working across organisational boundaries. Core competence applies to both manufacturing and services. Unlike physical assets, core competence does not diminish with use. Core competencies are enhanced as they are applied and shared. "Competencies are the glue that binds existing businesses. They are also the engine for new business development."[24] They guide diversification and new market entry. Prahalad and Hamel say few companies can build world leadership in more than five or six competencies.

A theory of competitive advantage built around core competence would rest on three links[25]:

- Core competence provides potential access to a variety of markets through core products and end products. For example, competence in display systems enables a company to be in such diverse businesses as calculators, miniature TV sets, monitors for laptop computers, and automotive dashboards.
- Core competence should contribute significantly to customer value/benefit in the end product. For example, Honda's core competence in engines.
- Core competence should be difficult for rivals to imitate. This will be the case if the core competence is built on a complex harmonisation of technologies and production skills. Competitors may be able to copy some of the technologies in the core competence but will find it difficult to duplicate the "competence system" as a whole and how it functions in an organisation.

If core competence has the elements to constitute a strategy, it would be corporate strategy and not business strategy. Porter in his industry analysis is talking about business strategy—ompeting at the business or SBU level. Porter believes real competition takes place at the operating level, not corporate level. He is not talking about strategy in a diversified corporation. He is talking about strategy at the SBU level—how various businesses compete in an industry. In core competence, Prahalad and Hamel are referring to strategy at the corporate level. They believe much of the problem with strategy is that corporations are fragmented into SBUs, each pursuing its own strategic designs with no central coordination or policy foundations. Competition should be between corporations. Corporate policies should provide the foundation for how the corporation as a whole wants to compete in the market. That foundation is core competence. It is the corporation that must decide what is its core competence.

Based on its core competence, end products are developed by the SBUs. Diversification into different products, businesses, and regions is guided by the company's core competence. Additional competencies needed to support the development of new end products are acquired if not already available within the corporation. All strategic decisions with regard to products and markets originate from the core competence of the corporation. Customer value and competitive advantage also come from core competence. Decisions on outsourcing and make-or-buy are guided by core competence. Corporations do not outsource or divest core competence or core products. Control of core products is critical because it is core products that spawn end products. The link between core competence, core products, and end products is key. All outside links, including strategic alliances, should be seen as opportunities to strengthen existing competencies or learn new competencies.

Prahalad and Hamel provide several case examples of companies that have built global leadership in their business based on their core competence. They cite Honda with its core competence in engines, 3M's competence in sticky tape, Sony in miniaturisation, Philip's optical media expertise, Citicorp in operating system, and Canon's core competence in optics, imaging, and microprocessor controls. Although some of the examples cited are dated, nevertheless they lend support to the point Prahalad and Hamel are trying to make—namely, companies should stop imagining themselves as bundles of businesses making products but rather as in a race to build competencies for present and future global leadership.

The core competence perspective of strategy development is not without problems. Its critics raise various difficulties with the concept. They point out that many of the successful companies today began in totally different businesses. Johnson & Johnson began as a supplier of antiseptic gauze and medical plasters and got into the body powder business by accident. Marriott began in the restaurant business. American Express was a freight express business. 3M was a mining company. These companies did not grow into their present businesses based on any particular core competence they had. Their shift into new business was incremental and opportunistic. They did not plan to become what they are today based on any analysis of their core competence or strength. There was no grand strategic plan in their minds when they made their moves. They just evolved and exploited opportunities that came their way.

Also, core competence has particular relevance to established, large corporations that are diversified. It is not relevant to start-up entrepreneurial ventures. Such businesses are too new to have any identifiable core competence. Their strategic path is likely to be more experimental and "try a lot of stuff". Core competence takes time to develop. There is also the added question of whether core competence is deliberately built by corporate leaders or whether it grows and emerges over time. It is not clear from the literature how a corporation acquires core competency. It is only argued that core competence should be the source of corporate strategy for growth and diversification.

There is also another problem. Core competence can become obsolete as a result of changes in customer needs or technology. Disruptive technology can make core competence irrelevant. Kodak was an iconic industry leader, synonymous with photography. Its core competence in film technology did not protect its leadership in the market when digital photography appeared. The new film technology made Kodak's core competence irrelevant. Similar developments have taken place in the PC business. Companies like IBM and GE have adapted to disruptive innovations and gone beyond core competence—leaving old businesses and entering new ones. To remain relevant, companies must be prepared to abandon even core products and markets of today and develop new core competencies to compete for the future.

Capabilities

While Prahalad and Hamel talk about competing on "core competence", George Stalk et al. talk about competing on "capabilities".[26] Although capabilities fall within the category of organisational resources and are therefore part of RBV, its proponents argue that capabilities differ from core competence. Core competence is more skill and technology related. Capabilities are organisational based—the unique ability to manage organisational practices and business processes to render superior value to customers. Capability is about managing organisational resources differently—including human resources and relationships with suppliers, customers, and strategic partners. Competitive advantage comes from organisational capabilities.

Stalk and his colleagues cite several examples of capabilities-based competition. They point out that the competitive advantage of Walmart comes from its "cross-docking" system of store management. They also argue that the success of Honda does not lie so much on its core competence in engines and power trains as posited by Prahalad and Hamel but more on its unique capability in "dealer management"—its "ability to train and support its dealer network for merchandising, selling, floor planning, and service management."[27] First developed in its motorcycle business, Honda has been able to replicate this business process in the new businesses the company has entered since.

Stalk et al. posit that capabilities-based competition rests on four principles[28]:

- The building blocks of corporate strategy are not products and markets but business processes.
- Competitive success depends on transforming a company's processes into strategic capabilities and consistently providing superior value to the customer.

- Companies create these capabilities by making strategic investments in a support infrastructure that links together and transcends traditional SBUs and functions.
- Because capabilities necessarily cross functions, the champion of a capabilities-based strategy is the CEO.

These four principles govern the capabilities framework to competitive advantage. The unit of analysis for strategy shifts from Porter's industry to the firm, but within the firm it concentrates on organisational processes and behaviour. For analysis, it relies more on organisation theory than economics. It has similarities with the core competence framework in that both look inside the organisation for understanding business strategy and competitive advantage rather than outside in industry structures. But capabilities insight concentrates more on firm-specific organisational elements that support competition. Core competence is concerned with identifying the core strength of the company and then developing products and markets based on its strength. However, capabilities and core competence as frameworks overlap in many areas of analysis and concern.

David Teece et al. have added another dimension to the RBV framework in their article "Dynamic Capabilities and Strategic Management."[29] In this article, they argue that to achieve sustainable competitive advantage firms need "dynamic capabilities." The dynamic capabilities framework analyses creating competitive advantage in an environment of rapid technological change—under Schumpeter's conditions of "creative destruction." Teece believes the dynamic capabilities paradigm offers a better theory of firm performance.

The dynamic capabilities insight takes off from the resource-based view of competition. RBV focusses on strategies for exploiting existing firm-specific resources. But it is also concerned with developing new capabilities to exploit new market opportunities or to cope with Schumpeter's creative destruction brought about by disruptive technologies. Dynamic capabilities focuses on the second aspect—developing new invisible assets of the corporation that go beyond accumulation of valuable technology assets. Technology assets alone are not enough to support competitive advantage. Companies need to develop firm-specific capabilities and competencies to respond to shifts in the business environment. Innovative responses are required when the rate of technological change is rapid and when future competition and markets are difficult to predict. Dynamic capabilities is concerned with addressing these issues.

Teece and his colleagues define dynamic capabilities as the "firm's ability to integrate, build, and configure internal and external competencies to address rapidly changing environments."[30] Dynamic capabilities are seen as embedded in organisational processes, which in turn are shaped by the firm's current assets and its evolutionary path. What the firm can do and where it can go is constrained by its asset position and its path dependencies. Its competitors likewise are constrained. Competitive advantage will come to the firm that has the capabilities to reconfigure and transform the processes, routines, skills, and complementary assets of the firm to make them distinct and difficult to imitate by rivals.

Whether the dynamic capabilities approach is a different paradigm from capabilities and core competence is open to discussion. All three have overlapping areas of analysis and concerns. Even Porter's and Barney's analyses are not static—they do deal with issues of change. In particular, capabilities and dynamic capabilities are very similar in their unit of analysis—organisational and managerial competence that can provide competitive advantage. Both see organisational processes and behaviour—the invisible assets—as the source for competition. Competitive advantage comes not from outside the firm (industry) but from within—its competence and ability to be creative and innovative and provide value to customers. Needed capabilities have to be built over time, either from within or obtained from the outside through acquisitions and strategic partnerships. Dynamic capabilities is different only in its emphasis. Since the business environment is constantly changing, the capabilities of the firm must also change and grow in order to remain competitive. Firm capabilities can become obsolete. Therefore there is a need for the firm to build dynamic capabilities to deal with changing competition and customer needs. A rigid set of capabilities inherited from the past will not suffice in a dynamic, competitive environment. The underlying concept in dynamic capabilities is how the firm can remain innovative and creative.

The concept of change and innovation is also found in core competence. Core competencies are not static. The core competence of a firm can lose its competitive advantage because of changes in technology, customer needs, or institutional constraints. When that happens, the existing core competence of the firm built from the past may no longer be relevant. At this point, the firm needs to build new core competencies to compete. A better strategy for the firm would be not to wait until it reaches the inflection point but to start building its competencies for the future. This is the logic of Prahalad and Hamel in their book **Competing For The Future**. The problem is: How do you predict the future? Drucker provides the answer—you create it. In their book, Prahalad and Hamel explain how corporations can dominate tomorrow's competition.

Notes

1. Rothaermel [2].
2. Wernerfelt [3].
3. Prahalad and Hamel [4].
4. Barney [5].
5. Penrose [6].
6. Barney [5, p. 106].
7. **Ibid**., p. 106.
8. **Ibid**., p. 102.
9. Jay Barney, **ibid**., pp. 105–106. See also his book Barney [7].
10. Barney [5, p. 102].
11. Grant [1, p. 117].
12. **Ibid**., p. 117.
13. **Ibid**., p. 117.

14. Bridoux [8].
15. Porter [9].
16. Piem and Butler [10].
17. Barney [5].
18. See Barney [11].
19. Prahalad and Hamel [4].
20. Barney [7, p. 135].
21. Prahalad and Hamel [4, p. 81].
22. **Ibid.**, p. 81.
23. **Ibid.**, pp. 81–82.
24. See **Ibid.**, p. 83.
25. Stalk et al. [12].
26. **Ibid.**, p. 65.
27. **Ibid.**, p. 60.
28. Teece et al. [13].
29. **Ibid.**, p. 516.

References

1. Grant R (1991) The resource—based theory of competitive advantage: implications for strategy formulation. California Manage Rev (Spring)
2. Rothaermel F (2013) Strategic management concepts. McGraw-Hill Irwin, p 8
3. Wernerfelt B (1984) A resource-based view of the firm. Strat Manage J 5(2) (April–June)
4. Prahalad CK, Hamel G (1990) The core competence of the corporation. Harvard Bus Rev (May–June)
5. Barney J (1991) Firm resources and sustained competitive advantage. J Manage 17(1)
6. Penrose E (1959) The theory of the growth of the firm. Wiley, New York
7. Barney J (2007) Chapter 5, Evaluating firm strengths and weaknesses: the resource—based view. In: Gaining and sustaining competitive advantage, 3rd edn. Pearson Education
8. Bridoux F (1997) A resource—based approach to performance and competition: an overview of the connections between resources and competition. Strat Manage J 5 (Summer, Special issue)
9. Porter M (1991) Towards a dynamic theory of strategy. Strat Manage J 12:108 (Winter, Special issue)
10. Piem R, Butler J (2001) Is the resource—based "view" a useful perspective for strategic management research? Acad Manage Rev 26(1)
11. Barney J (2001) "Is the resource—based "view" a useful perspective for strategic management research?" Yes. Acad Manage Rev 26(1)
12. Stalk G, Evans P, Schulman L (1992) Competing on capabilities: the new rules of corporate strategy. Harvard Bus Rev (March–April)
13. Teece D, Pisano G, Shuen A (1997) Dynamic capabilities and strategic management. Strat Manage J 18(7)

Chapter 5
The Third Leg of Strategy

Abstract In the study of strategy, Porter focuses on industry structure. Barney focuses on firm resources. Peng's third leg—institutions—is the focus of this chapter. Peng's argument is that institutions play a critical role in strategy formulation. They are more than 'background' factors. This chapter examines the role of institutions and national cultures in strategy formulation, with particular reference to developed, developing, and transition societies. The central idea is that strategy cannot be divorced from institutions and cultures. As institutions and cultures change, strategies also need to change. Strategy models make sense only in the context of institutions and cultures. Strategy models developed in the West with different institutions and cultures may not apply to other countries whose institutions and cultures are different. The chapter reviews the meaning of institutions, the impact of institutions on strategy, and the nexus between culture and strategy. There is discussion on how business decision making in emerging and transition societies differs from the West because of differences in institutions. This has important implications for Western corporations engaged in international business. Their successful strategies in the West may be totally irrelevant to competing in emerging and transition countries. The implicit assumption that strategies are generic and apply everywhere is not supported by research. Countries matter. Emerging and transition societies are changing. This means businesses operating in these societies will also need to change their strategies. These and similar issues and challenges form the core of the discussion in this chapter.

The strategy literature indicates there are different approaches to understanding strategy. Initially, the field was dominated by two paradigms—Porter's industry analysis and Barney's resource view. In the 1990s, a third perspective emerged—the institutional framework, championed by Mike Peng and others. In a 2009 article in the **Academy of Management** called "The Institution-Based View as a Third Leg for a Strategy Tripod",[1] Peng et al. spelled out the case for an institutional approach to strategy. The view presented was that strategy stands on three legs—industry structure (Porter), firm resources (Barney), and institutions (Peng) (Fig. 5.1).

© The Author(s), under exclusive license to Springer Nature Singapore Pte Ltd. 2021

L. Iruthayasamy, *Understanding Business Strategy*,
https://doi.org/10.1007/978-981-33-6542-1_5

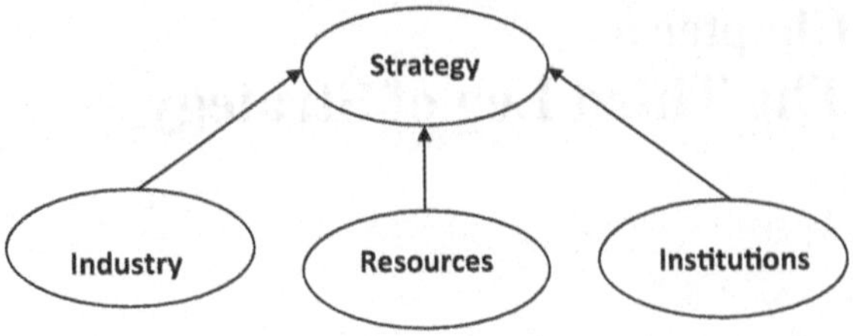

Fig. 5.1 The strategy tripod. *Source* Author

The institutional paradigm is not new. Porter's framework of strategy is built on the environment—forces external to the firm that shape the firm's strategy. The S-C-P paradigm—structure—conduct—performance—rests on the external environment as the unit of analysis. It is industry structure that determines firm conduct, which in turn determines firm performance. But the environment that Porter looks at is the task environment—more specifically, the industry in which the firm operates. Porter ignores or, at best, glosses over other elements in the environment that can and do shape the policies and economic performance of the firm. Apart from the role of government, which Porter acknowledges as impacting firm strategy and performance, his analysis does not include any systematic treatment of institutions in the environment that influence firm decisions and actions. Clearly, this is a gap in Porter's analysis of strategy. The institutional theory of strategy attempts to fill this gap.

The RBV paradigm is more explicit in acknowledging the importance and relevance of the environment on firm performance. Its basic approach is built on SWOT—matching the strengths and weaknesses of the firm with the threats and opportunities in the environment. But, as in the case of Porter, there is no explicit analysis of what elements in the environment impact firm performance and how. There is only a general recognition of the need for a "fit" between the resources of the firm and environmental opportunities and threats. The unit of analysis in RBV remains internal—organisational resources that can provide and sustain competitive advantage. The RBV too, like the S-C-P approach, has a gap in its analysis—lack of specific recognition of the impact of context and institutions on organisational strategy.

The literature on business strategy has always recognised, in a general way, the influence of the environment on firms. PESTEL has been part of strategy analysis for a long time. In particular, political, economic, and social forces in the environment have always been recognised as influencing business policies and decisions, especially in international business. With geographic diversification, the experiences of multinational companies have reinforced the significant impact different national environments have on business. Doing business in different countries is a challenge because the business environment is different. The rules of the game are different. Each national environment presents different opportunities, threats, and constraints. Doing business in China is quite different from doing business in Malaysia or Indonesia. Doing business in the West where formal institutions are well developed is different from doing business in emerging or transition economies where institutions are weak. Businesses operating in different institutional environments cannot develop winning strategies simply based on their unique internal resources (RBV) or the competitive forces in the industry in which they operate (Porter). They need a third leg to stand on—specific understanding of the institutions in the countries where they are operating and how these institutions create opportunities and constraints.

Business strategies cannot work if institutional constraints and opportunities are not specifically incorporated into the strategy-making process. The institutional framework of each country where the firm operates has to be identified and analysed and strategies and operations developed within the constraints imposed by the framework. Generic strategies developed in the home country without understanding the institutional framework of host countries are unlikely to work. Institutional theory seeks to provide the understanding needed to develop viable business strategies for companies operating in different countries with different institutional frameworks. It is only institutional analysis that can answer the fundamental question raised by Rumelt and his colleagues in 1994: Why do strategies of firms from different countries and regions differ?[2] The answer appears to be national culture and institutions.

Institutions

What constitutes the institutional framework of a country? Peng identifies two dimensions of institutions—formal and informal.[3] At the general level, formal institutions refer to the social, political, and economic framework of a country that conditions behaviour and transactions. In specific terms, they refer to regulatory mechanisms that influence social and business conduct, such as laws, regulations, policies, and practices that sanction what is acceptable and non-acceptable behaviour. The constraints are generally enacted by governments or are the product of historical evolution. Included are economic and political systems. Courts and legal processes that enforce laws are part of formal institutions. Douglas North defines institutions as "the rules of the game in a society; more formally, they are the humanly devised constraints that shape human interaction".[4] This includes business transactions. All businesses, both domestic and foreign, are required to play by these rules. The rules can be changed by the government and those who can influence the government. New rules can be enacted.

The laws and rules of the game can have a positive or negative impact on business. New tax laws and foreign exchange controls and policies on investments and profit repatriation can all have a critical effect on business operations and strategies. Both developed and emerging countries employ formal institutions to "regulate" what business can do and cannot do. In developed countries, formal institutions are more structured and their operations more transparent. The rules are more clearly established and understood. There are clear processes for changing the rules of the game. They cannot be arbitrarily changed. A certain rationality governs how these rules are established and why they are needed. Conflicts, both business and non-business, are resolved through court procedures. There are clear structures for enforcement of rules. These are the rule-based societies. The rules are transparent and are enacted through a legislative process. This process is part of the political culture that characterises developed countries in the West.

Given the ideological commitment to a free-market economy in the West, the preference is for fewer rules to regulate business. This partly explains the rise and success of entrepreneurship in countries like the United States. Entrepreneurship cannot thrive in an environment that is too constraining—too many rules and regulations kill creativity and innovation. While formal institutions are necessary to establish the rules of the game, their impact on business is kept to a minimum in the West. The idea is to let businesses grow and thrive through fair competition rather than through centralised control.

This commitment to free market forces in the West means institutions are not perceived to be that relevant to understanding business strategy. Institutions are seen as "background conditions", not as critical inputs for business decision making. This explains why the I/O and RBV approaches to business strategy pay so little attention to institutional theory. Institutions play a smaller role in business strategy in the West. Also, in the West institutions are more formal than informal. In emerging and transition societies, institutions, both formal and informal, are more significant in determining business policies and decision making. This explains why much of the work on institutional theory and its impact on business strategy have come from research done in emerging countries, especially Asian countries. In Asian countries, institutions are not background factors. They are fundamental to how business, both local and foreign, operate and take decisions.

As stated earlier, institutions can be formal or informal. In developed countries, formal institutions predominate. The business environment is rule-based. Business transactions and exchanges are governed by explicit laws, procedures, and policies that are transparent and applied uniformly across the board. Laws are enforced by courts. Business disputes are adjudicated in a fair and transparent manner. Laws are applied in a predictable and consistent way. This provides business the needed measure of certainty to plan ahead and take long-term strategic decisions. Businesses need not rely on special connections and relationships with regulatory authorities for favours and special treatment. The formal institutions regulate business transactions. Firms are free to pursue their own strategies to compete in the market, as long as they operate within the constraints imposed by formal institutions. In such a business environment, there is little need for informal institutions. Hence the reason why business strategy theories developed in the United States and Europe in general make little reference to institutions in their explanation of business competition and performance.

The business environment in emerging and transition societies is different. Here, formal institutions are less developed. They may exist in form—that is, laws, procedures, policies, and systems exist but they are not enforced. If enforced, they are not enforced impartially. Because of the weakness of formal institutions, informal institutions take over the function of formal institutions. Connections and relationships with public policy makers determine business decisions, strategy, and business success. In this environment, neither Porter's I/O model nor Barney's RBV theory is satisfactory in explaining business strategy or providing prescriptions for business performance. We need to look at institutional theory for explanations. This is critically important to multinational corporations engaged in international business, especially in emerging and transition economies.

Impact of Institutions on Strategy

How do institutions really affect business operations and strategy? Much of the ongoing research in institutional theory is concerned with understanding what institutions are and how they are evolving; how institutions impact specific decisions of business; and how MNCs can steer their operations and strategies in countries where formal institutions are weak and informal institutions dominate.

In developed countries, formal institutions provide the framework for business operations and competition. This does not mean connections and relationships are not important. American companies spent millions of dollars lobbying for government support that can give them competitive advantage over their rivals. They attempt to influence government policies and regulations that have an impact on business operations, so much so that many are highly critical of the close nexus between Washington and Wall Street. The Occupy Wall Street movement reflects this perception of big business in America. Business connections and relationships with policy makers are not confined to developing countries. They also exist in the developed West.

But in the West, these informal institutions do not determine business decisions and business conduct. Businesses operate not on the basis of "connections" and "relationships" but rules that all play by—the formal institutions. Those who do not play by the rules face consequences. The rules are transparent. There are mechanisms to change the rules. But once the rules are in place, everybody is required to play by the same rules. For example, the anti-trust laws in the United States ensure there is free competition and no collusion. The rules make possible a free market economy and competition. Businesses are free to develop strategies to compete, as long as they operate within the rules. The rules are kept to a minimum to provide the environment for entrepreneurial thinking and innovation.

In developed countries, the real challenge for business is to deal with market forces through innovative strategies. The I/O and RBV approaches to business strategy need to be understood in this context. The rationality and efficiency traits that characterise both these models are a reflection of the requirements of a free market economy. They are strategies to compete where market forces determine economic returns, not connections and personal relationships. This means the I/O and RBV based strategies will not apply to situations where market forces do not determine corporate outcomes. This is the case in most emerging and transition economies.

In developed societies, the primary function of formal institutions is to reduce uncertainty and provide a conducive environment for businesses to compete and grow. Formal institutions can be positive or negative. If they create uncertainty, they can impact businesses negatively. The Brexit decision is a classic example of an institutional change that has great potential consequences for businesses globally because it creates so much uncertainty. Uncertainty reduces the capacity of businesses to plan and take long-term strategic decisions. Strategy models assume a certain degree of stability in the environment. They are less predictive under conditions of turbulence. When existing economic, political, and social institutions break down, the resulting confusion and uncertainty makes it difficult for businesses to operate normally until new rules of the game are established. Institutions matter for business. Yet the two dominant business strategy models—I/O and RBV—have little to say on institutions and how they influence strategy.

The true impact of institutions on business and business strategy is more clearly discernible in emerging and transition societies. In these societies, formal institutions are under flux. They are not firmly established and are still evolving. Because formal institutions are weak, informal institutions become more dominant. They define the rules of the game and how businesses operate in these environments. Informal institutions refer to such things as norms, culture, ethics, beliefs, values, traditions, and practices of the society in which a business operates. These "intangibles" provide the framework for business operations and behaviour. They take the place of formal institutions or may work together with formal institutions that are slowly emerging, in which case there is a mixture of formal and informal institutions. This is the typical business environment in countries that are in transition.

Many countries in Asia, Eastern Europe, Latin America, and Africa fall in this category. The business environment in these countries provides unique challenges for businesses, both domestic and foreign. Multinational corporations from the West operating in these countries cannot simply replicate their business strategies from home and hope to succeed. Their successful strategies in the West may be totally irrelevant to competing in transition and emerging countries. There is an implicit assumption that business strategies—whether based on the I/O or RBV model—are generic. Strategy studies in different countries, especially in emerging markets, do not support this assumption. The studies support the thesis that countries matter. The business environment is different in different countries. Business needs to respond differently to different environmental challenges and constraints. This has important implications for companies involved in international business in terms of strategy and competition.

Specifically, how do country differences impact business strategy and operations? At the generic level, national culture is a key determinant. It is well established that countries differ in culture. The work of Hofstede, Trompenaars, Hampden-Turner, Andre Laurent, and others in cross-cultural management underscore the relationship between management and national culture.

No organisation can escape from the influence of national culture. All management is culture-bound. This includes business enterprises. It means national culture imposes certain constraints on what a business can do and should not do. Business strategies that are in conflict with cultural norms, beliefs, and values are unlikely to gain legitimacy. Legitimacy is important for business success. Without legitimacy, businesses cannot operate or may not be allowed to operate in any society. In developed countries, the legitimacy comes from the legal framework in place, i.e., from the formal institutions. In emerging countries where formal institutions are weak, legitimacy comes from informal institutions, of which national culture is a significant component. Irrespective of the source of legitimacy—formal or informal institutions—legitimacy is critical to business success. No business strategy can work that is not sanctioned by legitimacy.

An important part of business strategy involves adaptation, especially in international business. A successful business adapts its marketing mix to local market conditions. Its marketing strategy is about combining the 4Ps of marketing to offer value to customers. The objective of adaptation is not just economic. It is also to gain legitimacy. This is why McDonald's adapts its products to the Indian market—most Indians don't eat beef, and many are vegetarians. McDonald's cannot afford to ignore Indian cultural norms if it wants legitimacy. KFC serves rice in Asian countries for similar reasons. Companies doing business in Islamic countries ensure their products, operations, and strategies are "syariah" compliant. Again the reason is not just economic. It is also legitimacy—to obtain social acceptance of the business and its products in an Islamic environment. Culture, norms, and values are critically important when it comes to legitimacy. This is where institutional analysis becomes crucial to understanding business strategy. Business does not operate in a cultural vacuum. It is necessarily embedded in a country's history, traditions, norms, and values. There is globalisation, but countries and national culture are real. Businesses cannot ignore them or develop strategies without taking cognizance of them. In this context, it is institutional theory that provides important inputs for business strategy.

Culture and Strategy

There are studies that show specific links between national culture and business strategy, especially in international business (IB). Kogut and Singh in their article "The Effect Of National Culture On The Choice Of Entry Mode" discuss how national culture influences a firm's choice of entry.[5] A firm has various choices in terms of entry modes. The three principal entry modes are joint ventures (JVs), greenfield investments, and acquisitions. What determines the strategic choice? The argument of Kogut and Singh is that the culture of the country that a firm wants to enter significantly influences the choice. The choice is not just based on industry transaction cost analysis. Cultural and institutional factors play an important role in the decision. Different countries have different propensities for joint ventures, greenfields, and acquisitions. Studies show that the frequency of oversees joint ventures among American companies is lower than European companies. On foreign acquisitions, there is significant difference in pattern among American, British, and Japanese corporations. There is a relationship between a firm's country of origin and the mode of entry. Japanese, Scandinavian, and French companies lean toward joint ventures. United Kingdom prefers acquisitions. Apart from joint ventures, Japanese firms appear to be comfortable with greenfield investments. There is a country pattern in entry modes.

The explanation posited is that the choice of entry mode is significantly influenced by the culture of the home country. Culture is not the only factor determining foreign entry mode, but it is an important influence. The cultural influence works through the home country's attitude towards uncertainty and uncertainty avoidance. Uncertainty impacts on investment decisions, specifically on the ability of the foreign firm to manage local operations of its subsidiaries. The perceived ability to manage foreign operations depends on the cultural attitude toward uncertainty avoidance. Firms coming from countries with high uncertainty avoidance traits look to do business with countries that are culturally similar or select an entry mode to minimise managing uncertainty.

Kogut and Singh employ the concept of psychic and cultural distance to analyse entry mode decisions. Psychic and cultural distance increase uncertainty and cost of doing business. Acquisitions and greenfield investments in a foreign market that is culturally different from the home market increase uncertainty. To minimize uncertainty, a firm that comes from a culture characterised by uncertainty avoidance will choose joint venture as the mode of entry. Acquisition and greenfield pose more uncertainties in managing the firm's investments. In this context, cultures of home and host countries significantly influence both the choice of countries for investment and the mode of investment. While many factors drive the foreign investment decision of a firm, cultural distance between the home and host country plays an important role in the decision. This explains why countries prefer to do business with countries that are similar to them, similar in terms of culture and institutions.

But is it "national culture" or "national institutions" that really matters? Kulwant Singh in his article "The limited value of culture to strategy" argues that culture has limited relevance for strategy.[6] He goes on to say, "Specifically, culture provides very limited explanation for variance in firm behavior or performance."[7] Culture is too broad a concept to explain any particular organisational phenomenon. Incorporating culture has not helped to explain variation of firm performance. "Culture is largely irrelevant for firm strategy."[8]

Asian business characteristics such as ownership structures, inter-firm relationships within diversified groups, and supplier relationships and networks are not unique to Asia. They are also found elsewhere. The characteristics are not due to differences in national culture but to differences in national institutions. Business structures such as "keiretsu" in Japan, "chaebol" in Korea, and Chinese family businesses in Southeast Asia are not cultural in nature but rather the result of the failure of institutions to provide the rules of the game for business competition. There is little evidence for any reliable association between economic success and national culture, or how culture influences firm strategy and performance.

The tendency to attribute the success of East Asian countries to "Asian culture", in particular to "Confucian values", rests on shaky grounds. Singh argues there is no rigorous evidence of culture's influence on firm strategy and performance in Asian countries. He also points out that certain cultural elements are found across countries. For example, there are studies that show the presence of Confucian values in the United States and Protestant work ethics in Malaysia. The correlation between national culture and performance, whether at the country or firm level, is nebulous.

Hence, Singh concludes with "the impact of a country's culture on firm strategy is relatively unimportant, both in Asia and more generally."[9]

It is to be noted that Singh does not dismiss culture altogether. He says, "It is not my position that culture has no impact on strategy."[10] He accepts that culture impacts every aspect of society in general, but for this very reason it cannot explain anything in particular. Culture is better "conceptualized as a background institution which frames or moulds other institutions, which then impact strategy more directly."[11] He adds "Culture-based explanations of firm-level performance can augment institution-based perspectives, but not replace them."[12]

Singh provides an alternative explanation to the culture argument for firm behaviour and performance. The alternative explanation is institutions. He writes:

> The importance of cooperative relationships or family ties for businesses in Asia and other emerging economies is due to the underdevelopment of institutions and markets rather than to cultural factors. Ethnic business networks in Asia are explained by inadequate markets, corrupt governments, weak legal systems, poor financial and banking sectors, and the absence of reliable intermediaries, rather than by culture … Business groups and diversification in emerging economies may be responses to market and institutional underdevelopment, not reflections of cultural values.[13]

Singh is not alone in his assessment of culture. Peng comes to a similar conclusion. With respect to entrepreneurship in China, Peng says "the emergence of entrepreneurship in mainland China seems to indicate that it is the development of market-supporting institutions, both formal and informal, that gives birth to a new wave of entrepreneurship… it is institutional frameworks, rather than national cultures, that drive entrepreneurship."[14]

The debate whether it is culture or institutions that influence business behaviour and strategy maybe a moot point. Even critics of the culture argument recognise that formal institutions are embedded in national cultures. Institutions combine formal and informal constraints to regulate how the game of business is played. The two components cannot be separated. Formal institutions rest on a body of beliefs and values, which is culture. For example, American capitalism, which is part of formal institution, is founded on the American value of economic freedom. Capitalism is therefore both institution and culture.

In trying to understand how institutions affect business behaviour and strategy, it is more fruitful not to be distracted by the culture debate but to concentrate on developing a more robust institutional theory as the third leg of strategy. Culture will always be part of national institutions. Culture provides the framework within which institutions function. The global manager engaged in IB must understand that institutions in the host country may appear to be the same as his own country. Such appearances can be deceptive. The institutions, though similar, can function differently because they rest on a different set of foundations, beliefs, and values—in other words, they are culturally different. The IB manager can only understand institutions in the host country if he understands the culture of the host country. An important objective of institutional theory should be to understand national culture and how it shapes the evolution of institutions in the country. Even in the developed West, institutions rest on Western civilisation, values, and modes of thinking.

To be fair to the culture critics, there is evidence that as market institutions develop in a country, business behaviour does change. Traditional modes of doing business—for example, connections and relationships—slowly get replaced by more rational and strategic thinking.

This phenomenon can be observed in China and other emerging countries. "Guanxi" is generally accepted as an important part of doing business in China. It is believed to rest on Confucian culture and values. According to Guthrie, it involves "the exchange of gifts, favours and banquets; the cultivation of personal relationships and networks of mutual dependence; and the manufacturing of obligation and indebtness."[15] Guanxi is defined as an institution providing an alternative path to Chinese bureaucratic procedures and processes, as a "shortcut around, or a coping strategy for dealing with bureaucratic power."[16] Guanxi makes it possible for businesses to operate by relying on connections instead of state organisational structures. Although there is debate on whether guanxi in China is declining, Gutherie's view is that the practice of guanxi is fading and increasingly becoming irrelevant as economic reforms progress. This does not mean trust and relationships are not important. Social relations will always remain relevant in business transactions, but guanxi will not be a business strategy as in the past. As the Chinese government loosens its control over the economy and establishes structures that are more rational-legal, the role of guanxi is expected to decline. As state capitalism and cronyism declines, the practice of guanxi will also decline. Business decisions will be based more on strategic considerations.

Guanxi emerged as a business practice because of the absence of business-supporting institutions. The role of guanxi in business is declining as formal market institutions emerge. In other words, culture is giving way to institutions as drivers of business strategy. This does not mean Confucian culture with its emphasis on interpersonal kinship relations and clan systems will disappear from the Chinese business environment. It will remain, but only in the background, as an invisible hand underpinning business operations and strategy. It will be institutions, not culture, that will provide the operational framework for domestic and foreign business in China. Meanwhile, during the transition to modernisation, both guanxi and institutions will remain relevant to business in China.

This evolution from relationships and connections to institutions is a phenomenon observable in all transition and emerging countries. The IB manager needs to understand this evolution in his choice of business strategies to pursue. The I/O and RBV models alone will not provide him this understanding. He needs to look at the third leg of strategy—institutions to gain the strategic insight that he needs.

The full impact of institutions on business behaviour requires understanding that goes beyond national culture. When we say countries matter in business, we primarily mean institutions matter in business.[17] Institutions vary with countries. In developed countries, market and business institutions are well developed. The institutions function to regulate business to ensure everybody plays by the same rules. The rules are kept to a minimum to encourage business entrepreneurship and innovation. Factor markets ensure businesses have access to resources. Information is available for business decision making. Markets determine business performance. In this free market environment, businesses compete on the basis of strategies that give the highest return on investments. Institutions function to increase efficiency and reduce transaction cost for business.

In the business environment in developed counties, business strategies may be inspired by different modes of thinking—Porter's industry analysis, Barney's firm resources, Mintzberg's emergent strategy, Quinn's incrementalism or some other frameworks. But they all rest on a common foundation—free market forces and a set of institutions that provides a measure of certainty and legitimacy for business decision making. When this foundation is absent, the strategy models developed in the West lose their relevance and do not apply. This is the case in emerging economies. In these countries, formal institutions are just emerging. They are weak and at different stages of evolution. The state is strong. Many businesses are state enterprises. Business regulation is pervasive. There is lack of transparency in decision making by regulatory bodies. The government bureaucracy is inefficient and corrupt. Power is in the hands of a small group of ruling elites. There is a close nexus between business and government. Information is controlled. The judiciary is weak, corrupt, or controlled by elites. NGOs are weak or nonexistent to check abuses of power. Business opportunities are plentiful for those who have the right "connections." Business—supporting institutions may exist but they do not function as intended and therefore do not provide confidence to businesses. Political and social tensions are high because of lack of democratic institutions.

How do businesses operate in countries with these institutional characteristics? Do American theories of strategy apply? The existing strategy models—mostly developed in America—rest on institutional frameworks found in developed countries. They have little relevance for countries with different institutions. Firms, whether domestic or foreign, operating in emerging economies need to learn to operate within the institutional frameworks found in these countries. Domestic firms may find it easier to do this, as they are more familiar with their own environment. Foreign firms, especially from the developed West, will find the adaptation more difficult. Their successful strategy models in their home markets may not work in the host countries. The approach for them is to adapt the strategy models of the West to the national environments of the host countries. Here, the foreign firms may have a lot to learn from how the local businesses compete. But, they face a dilemma. Do they do what the domestic companies do, which will take them away from their home country strategies, or do they follow their home country strategies which may not work in the local environment? The corporate manager in IB has to resolve this challenge.

Businesses have developed strategies to cope with environments where formal institutions are weak. For example, foreign firms in IB choose entry modes that can reduce uncertainty. They tend to avoid acquisitions and greenfield investments because of lack of institutions that can protect their investments. They prefer joint-ventures and let their local partners deal with the uncertain local business environment. The choice of entry mode is influenced by the degree of institutional development in the host country and the uncertainty avoidance traits of the investor. The I/O or RBV model is not of much help in this decision making process. Hoskisson et al. confirm this observation when they say, "in the early stages of market emergence, institutional theory is preeminent in helping to explain impacts on enterprise strategies."[18] This is the conclusion they arrive at after exploring three perspectives on business strategy in emerging economies, namely, institutional theory, transaction cost economics, and the resource-based view of the firm.

The observation of Hoskisson et al. on institutional theory is particularly relevant to the question: What determines the scope of the firm? By scope is meant both geographic and product diversification. In an environment where formal institutions are weak, firms engaged in IB tend to diversify into countries that are culturally similar in order to reduce uncertainty in business behaviour and conduct. Cultural distance is an important concept in the internationalisation process of a firm. Firms further reduce risk and uncertainty by selecting certain entry modes over others. They prefer joint ventures to acquisitions or greenfield ventures because of the absence of institutional protection for their investments. In the case of product diversification, firms in environments where institutions are weak tend to move in the direction of conglomerate—they diversify into unrelated businesses. This is contrary to business strategies in developed countries where the emphasis is on focus and divesting unrelated businesses and products.

What explains this difference in strategy? The presence of strong functional institutions encourages growth through internal expansion and acquisition. Growth is the response to competition and a level playing field, but it is growth that is the product of careful planning and strategic thinking. Systematic growth is not possible without a functioning market and a legal framework that provides for efficient resource allocation, reduce transaction cost, and increase certainty. Peng and Heath make the point that it is difficult for firms in transition economies to grow internally or through mergers and acquisitions because of institutional constraints—lack of property rights and unstable political structures. Transition market firms tend to use "networks" as an alternative. They argue that by "pooling and coordinating resources, economies of scale and scope can be achieved and organizational learning can occur."[19] Networks help to fill the void created by the absence of institutions.

Another alternative mode of growth chosen by emerging and transition market firms is unrelated diversification—a strategy of conglomerates, also called "business groups" or "family businesses". This goes against mainstream strategic thinking in the West with its emphasis on focus and core competence. Conglomerates seem to work and provide value in emerging markets.

What explains the emergence and success of conglomerates in emerging economies? The traditional explanation is culture. The argument is that certain cultures are collective, like Asian culture. In collective cultures, people and firms have a propensity to work together in groups and families. For example, overseas Chinese family businesses in East and South East Asia are a product of Confucian culture and values with its emphasis on family and filial obligations. Therefore it is natural for Chinese firms to collaborate and network across industries and even countries based on "guanxi" and family ties. This often leads to a diversified business empire, headed by a founding family. This form of diversification leading to massive conglomerates are found in many Asian countries. Such conglomerates are not confined to Chinese. They are also found among other Asian ethnic groups, but the Chinese business networks stand out prominently. A good example would be the Salim group in Indonesia.[20] It was a huge conglomerate that dominated business in Indonesia during the Suharto regime, with tentacles stretching to other countries in the region.

The second explanation for a strategy of conglomerate in emerging and transition markets comes from institutional theory and transaction cost economics. Peng in his article "Towards an Institution-Based View of Business Strategy" states that in emerging economies formal institutions are unable to support low transaction-cost business operations because of the absence of: (1) a credible legal framework, (2) a stable political structure, and (3) functioning strategic factor markets.[21] Because of the weaknesses of formal institutions in these areas, "informal constraints rise to play a larger role in regulating economic exchanges in these countries during the transition."[22] The informal constraints come from three sources: interpersonal relations; external connections; and reputation of conglomerates. Although managers everywhere network, managers in emerging economies in Asia rely heavily on personal relationships for information on market opportunities because such information is not publicly available. Through such networking and personal relationships, managers in diversified conglomerates are able to reduce uncertainty in their strategic decision making. In countries with functioning formal institutions, such reliance on networking and personal relations for public information is not necessary.

External links with key stakeholders, especially government officials, are an important part of informal institution. Corporate managers maintain a "disproportionately greater contact" with government officials to cope with environmental uncertainty. Such government contacts have significant impacts on firm performance. For firms operating in institutionally unstable environments, "political sources" and "institutional capital" can be critical for success. Conglomerates learn to leverage their government contacts. Bribes, gifts, cronyism, and other corrupt practices become part of working with the public bureaucracy. Those practices serve an important functional role—they help businesses operate when formal institutions are absent or weak.

The reputation of conglomerates serves as an important informal element in reducing uncertainty for stakeholders. In emerging markets, independent consumer protection organisations are rare or ineffective. Consumers rely on the reputation of firms. Large and powerful conglomerates enjoy high reputation, which is leveraged to enter new industries and attract new capital for more growth. Reputation of conglomerates helps reduce transaction costs for external investors where public sources of information on firm performance are not readily available or reliable because of the absence of developed capital markets. This relationship between formal institutions and unrelated diversification seems to hold even in developed countries like the United States. Longitudinal studies show that investor sentiments toward conglomerates in the United States in the 1960s was positive compared to the 1980s because of differences in the capital market, specifically the availability of information for investment decisions. What is observed today in emerging economies with respect to conglomerates holds true for the United States when formal financial institutions were less developed.[23]

Peng in his paper says firms adopt three strategies for growth: generic expansion, mergers and acquisitions, and networks and alliances.[24] The choice appears to be governed by the institutional environment in which a firm operates. Generic expansion and mergers and acquisitions are difficult in markets where formal institutions are weak. The prerequisites for the strategies are not there. Generic expansion requires capable managers. Mergers and acquisitions need a functioning factor market. These conditions do not exist in transition and emerging economies. Consequently, firms tend to opt for the third growth strategy—networks and alliances. The third strategy does not rely on formal institutions. It is informal in nature and is based on interpersonal relations. Hence the importance of joint ventures, alliances, and conglomerates as growth strategies in emerging economies. These strategies rely on trust and personal relationships in business transactions and exchanges. Formal institutions are not critical to these forms of strategies. To quote Peng, "the failure of formal institutional frameworks has led to the reliance on informal constraints, which results in a network-based strategy."[25] The evidence suggests that as formal institutions develop, growth strategies pursued by firms change accordingly.

Guthrie talks about the declining influence of "guanxi" in China. As China embarks on institutional reforms, the practice of guanxi is declining. Legal and institutional reforms are changing business behaviour, especially in the urban industrial economy. Although there is still debate about the importance of guanxi, there is growing evidence that guanxi is becoming less significant for business success in China today. As one Chinese manager interviewed by Guthrie put it: "In the past, guanxi was really important in the business world. But now quality, price, speed and production seem to be all that matter. This is really the greatest achievement of the economic reform."[26] In other words, Chinese firms are switching to competitive strategies, away from networking and personal relationships.

Part of the reason why Chinese firms resort to a network-based strategy is culture. There is a cultural propensity for Chinese managers to network, unlike managers in the West. But this is only part of the explanation for such behaviour because network-based strategy is also found in other countries where there is no Chinese cultural influence, such as the Czech Republic, Hungary, and Russia. To quote Peng "… despite the lack of the cultural affinity between these Eastern European firms and their Chinese counterparts, their behaviour is remarkably similar."[27] Clearly, national culture is not an adequate explanation for this phenomenon. Similarities in institutional conditions provide a stronger explanation. Similar institutional environments seem to influence firms to adopt the same strategies for growth. It needs to be pointed out that while Western firms like IKEA and the Swedish truck maker Scania also engage in network-based strategies, the relationships within such groups are different in structure, ownership, and management from those in China, Japan, Korea, and Asia. In the West, business relationships are largely at arm's length.

Similar changes are taking place in supplier strategies in countries like Japan. The supply management system in Japan has been built around keiretsu networks—specifically, vertical keiretsus where manufacturing companies develop close network relationships with a select group of suppliers. The major automobile companies like Toyota, Nissan, and Honda are classic examples of companies with such supplier relationships. Vertical keiretsus built on trust and loyalty were effective supplier strategies at one time. Now, with globalisation and increased pressure to reduce costs, supplier strategies built on keiretsu are no longer cost-effective. The new competitive environment is forcing Japanese manufacturers to open up the supply chain. The keiretsu system, which has been so much a part of Japanese culture, is giving way because of institutional changes in the global business environment.[28]

Carlos Ghoshan in Nissan started the process of openness in purchasing and moving toward Western-style supplier relationship. He was accused of being un-Japanese, but his strategic change paid off. This prompted the other automobile players like Honda and Toyota to review the keiretsu system of supply chain management. The keiretsu system has not disappeared altogether in Japan, but the direction for an open purchasing policy is strong. Japanese companies are reengineering their keiretsus to increase competitiveness, including using global mega-suppliers. The reason for this strategic change is institutional and technological. Keiretsus had developed partly because of the Japanese propensity to cooperate, which is rooted in Japanese culture. But a more important reason for keiretsus is institutional. Although institutional reforms based on the American model were introduced after the War, these were not widely used. The Japanese tended to rely more on informal constraints, such as trust and relationship, instead of formal contracts. But now further institutional developments like globalisation, cost-cutting, and foreign pressure to open the Japanese market to global competition are forcing Japanese firms to either move away from the keiretsu system of supplier strategies or restructure the system to meet the needs of the new competitive environment.

Countries and country differences matter in strategy. The country differences are a combination of culture and institutions. The global manager in IB cannot afford not to take cognizance of the country differences in his pursuit of a profitable strategy. Strategy models formulated in the developed West with different cultures, institutions, and histories are unlikely to work in societies with different cultures and institutions. Institutions, in their various forms, act as formal and informal constraints to business behaviour. They also provide legitimacy to business actions. Businesses cannot ignore these constraints and legitimacies. Family business groups and conglomerates in South and East Asia, guanxi in China, keiretsu in Japan, and chaebols in Korea are business responses to specific institutional conditions and market imperfections. As these countries grow and reform and develop modern institutions and market structures, business strategies in these countries will also change and adapt accordingly[29]. The relevance of any specific strategy model depends on the institutional conditions of the host country. For strategies to work, they must be in alignment with local cultures, institutions, and aspirations. This poses a dilemma for global companies. How much do you localise? How much do you globalise? Each company has to resolve this challenge for itself. The decision is complex and involves many issues, including ethics. Think global, act local maybe too simplistic a solution.

Notes

1. Peng et al. [1].
2. Mentioned in Peng [2].
3. See Peng [3].
4. North [4]. Also see Peng [2]. Peng quotes Davis and North on institutions "as the set of fundamental political, social and legal ground rules that establishes the basis for production, exchange, and distribution."
5. Kogut and Singh [5].
6. Singh [6].
7. **Ibid**., p. 421.
8. **Ibid**., p. 422.
9. **Ibid**., p. 424.
10. **Ibid**., p. 425.
11. **Ibid**., p. 425.
12. **Ibid**., p. 425.
13. **Ibid**., p. 425.
14. Peng [2].
15. Quoted in Guthrie [7].
16. **Ibid**., p. 257.
17. See Makino et al. [8].
18. Hoskisson et al. [9].
19. Peng and Heath [10].
20. See Dieleman and Sachs [11].
21. Peng [2].
22. Quoted in **ibid**., p. 257.
23. See **ibid**., p. 258.
24. **Ibid**., p. 259.
25. **Ibid**., p. 260.
26. Douglas Guthrie, **op.cit**., p. 274.
27. Peng [12].
28. For a discussion of the changing Keiretsu system, see Aoki and Lennefors [13].
29. For a discussion of value loss arising from chaebols as a business organisation and strategy, see Ferris et al. [14].

References

1. Peng M, Sun SL, Pinkham B, Chen H (2009) The institution-based view as a third leg of strategy. Acad Manag 23(3)
2. Peng M (2002) Towards an institution-based view of business strategy. Asia Pac J Manag 19(2):251, 252, 255–257
3. Peng M (2006) Global strategy. In: Chapter 4: Emphasizing institutions, cultures, and ethics. Thomson South-Western

4. North D (1992) Transaction costs, institutions, and economic performance. International Center for Economic Growth, Occasional Papers, no. 30, p 5
5. Kogut B, Singh H (1988) The effect of national culture on the choice of entry mode. J Int Bus Stud 19(3)
6. Singh K (2007) The limited relevance of culture to strategy. Asia Pac Manag 24(4)
7. Guthrie D (1998) The declining significance of Guanxi in China's economic transition. China Q 154:256
8. Makino S, Isobe T, Chan C (2004) Does country matter? Strateg Manag J 25(10)
9. Hoskisson R, Eden L, Lau CM, Wright M (2000) Strategy in emerging economies. Acad Manag J 43(3):252
10. Peng M, Heath P (1996) The growth of the firm in planned economies in transition: institutions, organizations, and strategic choice. Acad Manag Rev 21(2):514
11. Dieleman M, Sachs W (2006) The Salim group: oscillating between a relationship-based and a market-based model. Asia Pac J Manag 23:(4)
12. Peng M (1997) Firm growth in transitional economies: three longitudinal cases from China, 1989–96. Org Stud 18(3):403
13. Aoki K, Lennefors TT (2013) The new, improved keiretsu. Harv Bus Rev 91
14. Ferris S, Kim K, Kitsabunnarat P (2003) The costs (and benefits?) of diversified business groups: the case of Korean Chaebols. J Bank Finance 27(2)

Chapter 6
Blue Ocean Versus Red Ocean

Abstract This Chapter presents and analyses the precepts and principles of blue ocean strategy (BOS) as championed by Kim and Mauborgne. BOS is the newest strategy model to be added to the strategy literature, with its own theory on strategy formulation and implementation. The chapter discusses what BOS is, how it differs from the other strategy approaches, does it offer any unique solutions to business problems, or is it just a passing fad. These issues are critically examined. The basic tenet of BOS is to avoid competition (red ocean) or make competition irrelevant. To be profitable, businesses need to find uncontested market space (blue ocean). Uncontested market space is found through value creation. BOS provides the analytical frameworks and tools to create value for the customer and the firm. The chapter includes discussion of specific BOS concepts like strategy canvas, value curve, value innovation and the four action framework. The eight principles for strategy formulation and implementation are also covered. Finally and importantly, the chapter raises the question: What is the contribution of BOS to strategic thinking and practice? Is it a new paradigm or just fluff? The claims of BOS are critically assessed for validity and its limitations pointed out. The major challenges that BOS has to contend with are identified and discussed. The chapter concludes by asserting that BOS is fine, provided it is not peddled as the solution to business strategy making.

Blue ocean strategy is the brainchild of two INSEAD professors—W. Chan Kim and Renée Mauborgne. Their ideas were first presented in an HBR article in 1997—"Value Innovation: The Strategic Logic of High Grow."[1] Subsequently, they refined their ideas and analysis in their two books published in 2005 and 2015. Today, blue ocean strategy occupies a significant place in the strategy literature, largely due to INSEAD adopting the concept as its flagship and incorporating it as a fundamental component in all its programmes, especially in its executive education and training courses. Blue Ocean Strategy Institutes have sprung up across countries to teach and apply its concepts and tools to analyse and solve problems in business, government, and social institutions. The Malaysian government has adopted blue ocean strategy as its fundamental framework for its Eleventh Malaysia Plan. The methodologies of blue ocean strategy are being applied to tackle problems in the public bureaucracy. Universiti Sains Malaysia, a premier public university in the country, has committed

© The Author(s), under exclusive license to Springer Nature Singapore Pte Ltd. 2021

L. Iruthayasamy, *Understanding Business Strategy*,
https://doi.org/10.1007/978-981-33-6542-1_6

itself to deploying the tools of blue ocean strategy to upgrade itself and its ranking as a global education provider. The university has published its ongoing experiences with blue ocean strategy in a book—"Blue Ocean Strategy Insights and Experiences of Universiti Sains Malaysia."[2]

What is blue ocean strategy? How does it differ from the other strategies discussed earlier? Does it offer any unique solutions to business performance, growth, and sustainability? These are important questions before business and non-business organisations start experimenting with blue ocean strategy. Blue ocean strategy has to be more than a passing fad.

The basic tenet of blue ocean strategy is quite simple, at least in the business world—avoid competition or make competition irrelevant. The argument is that competition is not good for business profitability or growth. Competition erodes profits and ultimately leads to price war. This is a race to the bottom, which does not benefit business or the customer for that matter. To be profitable and to grow, businesses need to find uncontested market space—i.e., markets where there are no competitors.

The I/O model of Porter is for a contested market—how to beat your rivals in a competitive industry. It is competition based. Blue ocean strategy is non-competitive. It is about avoiding competition or making competition irrelevant. Companies in the Porter's framework compete in the bloody red ocean where competition is fierce. It is difficult to win in the red ocean because of the intensity of competition. Competition forces profits down. Revenue and market share decline. Companies benchmark against each other in products, services, and strategy. They become similar. Some may be able to differentiate themselves through different business models and strategies and earn higher returns, but for most the red ocean is not profitable. For them, the only way to be successful is to move to the blue ocean where there is no competition. You make more money in an uncontested market. This, in a nutshell, is blue ocean versus red ocean.

Generally, uncontested market space is found in monopolies of one form or another. Governments can create monopolies for various reasons—for example, to protect nascent industries from foreign competition. Monopolies may be created for reasons of national security. In many emerging countries, monopolies are created to favour and protect cronies of those in power. Uncontested market space can also be the result of enforcing intellectual property rights, such as patents. Conceptually, blue ocean strategy is about the same thing—creating monopoly power, but monopoly power that is created deploying a different set of tools from government actions and patents. But the underlying idea is the same—to monopolise a market, or, at least, reduce competition.

The books and articles on blue ocean strategy are all about how a business can get away from competition by looking for uncontested markets. Uncontested markets are created. They are created by management decisions and actions. The fundamental prerequisite for this is a different business mindset—a mindset that thinks differently from the prevailing norms in the industry. It is divergent thinking—divergent from the conventional wisdoms of competing in a market.

Blue ocean strategy is visualization—visualising a new way of competing and doing business. It calls for the "mind of the strategist" of Kenichi Ohmae where imagination, intuition, and creativity come together. But the starting point of strategic thinking is analysis. Strategic thinking cannot happen in a vacuum. It is the analysis that drives the thinking process. Kim and Mauborgne in their writings lay down the analytical frameworks and tools for blue ocean thinking and implementation.

If blue ocean strategy is about uncontested market space, the foundation for that is what the authors call "value innovations." You create uncontested market by creating value for the customer and the firm. They call value innovation the "cornerstone of blue ocean strategy."[3] And value is created through "the simultaneous pursuit of differentiation and low cost."[4] You keep competitors away by creating value that competitors cannot create. You do this by deploying certain analytical frameworks and tools.

The Strategy Canvas and Value Curve

To develop a blue ocean strategy (create uncontested market space), you must first understand the existing industry and how the game of competition is being played. You must understand the terrain and how companies presently compete. Strategy canvas is a diagnostic and action tool to analyse and understand how companies presently compete in the industry and how value is created. Blue ocean strategy is about reconfiguring competition in the industry. The objective is to reduce cost and increase value for the customer without a trade-off between the two. High value and low cost can be achieved simultaneously.

To reduce cost and increase value simultaneously, the firm has to create a unique "value curve" for itself. The firm's value curve must be different from its competitors and the industry. The value curve of the firm is what differentiates the firm from its competitors and the industry. The value curve depicts a firm's relative performance across the industry's factors of competition. Companies competing in the red ocean tend to have converging value curves when plotted on the strategy canvas, which means they essentially have the same strategic profile. In other words, they perform in similar ways across the key factors for success in the industry. They are "all different in the same way." This is the result of firms benchmarking competitors and trying to outperform each other by "offering a little more for a little less." Blue ocean strategy is fundamentally shifting the strategy canvas of the industry—competing in totally new ways.

In their writings, Kim and Mauborgne cite several companies that successfully developed value curves that differentiated them from their competitors in the industry. In their 1997 article on value innovation, they discuss a number of companies that structured unique value curves to beat their competitors—Bert Claeys, Accor, Virgin Group, Compaq, and CNN. Bert Claeys, a Belgian company in the movie theatre business, found itself in a declining industry in the 1980s, with many cinema operators forced to shut down. Those who survived turned their cinemas into multiplexes.

But Bert Claeys did not follow the industry trend. Instead, it created Kinepolis, the world's first megaplex. It was neither a cinema nor a multiplex. It offered cinema goers a radically superior experience. In creating Kinepolis, Bert Claeys made its competition irrelevant because it provided its customers a quantum leap in value. It did not benchmark against competitors but transcended industry conditions. Kinepolis achieved profitable growth through reducing cost and increasing value. This is a blue ocean strategic move.

Accor, a French budget hotel company, was in trouble in the 1980s because the budget hotel industry was suffering from stagnation and overcapacity. In 1985 Accor broke from the industry and created a quantum leap in value for its customers when it launched Formulae 1 with a unique value curve which offered "unprecedented value to the mass of budget hotel customers in France by giving them much more of what they need most and much less of what they are willing to do without."[5] Formulae 1's value curve was significantly different from the industry value curve. The company reconfigured its performance across the industry's key success factors. This is blue ocean move. In red ocean, firms tend not to challenge the shape of the industry value curve. At best, they may offer a little more for a little less. They do not create fundamentally new and superior value curves. Accor not only captured the mass of French budget-hotel customers but also attracted new customers in the form of truck drivers who had previously not used budget hotels. This is one of the guiding principles of blue ocean strategy—go after the mass market and noncustomers. Red ocean competition is different. It relies on market segmentation and niche customers.

Virgin Atlantic Airways is another example discussed in the article on value innovation. The airline challenged industry logic by eliminating first-class service in 1984 and channeling the savings to increase value for business-class passengers through product and service innovation. First class was a big cost generator, while industry's profitability came from business class. The airline saw value innovation in the business class. It raised seat comfort for business-class passengers beyond industry standards. It also provided free transportation to and from the airport. These value innovations attracted new customers to the airlines—economy and first-class passengers who saw value in the business class offered by the airline. When the value curves of the competitors began to converge with Virgin's value curve, the airline went for a new leap in value innovation. It made a strategic move to provide lounges in airports for business passengers to rest and refresh themselves while they waited for connecting flights. The lounges also had state-of-the-art office equipment so that busy executives could use their waiting time productively. Virgin's decision to abandon the first class segment was a challenge to conventional industry wisdom. Virgin's value innovation lay in conceiving its business in terms of providing total solution to customer problems.

The article also discussed CNN and Compaq as value innovators. In 1980 CNN revolutionised television news by creating a quantum leap in value, not by competing with the networks but by replacing the network's format with real-time news around the world 24 h a day. CNN became the leader in global news broadcasting by finding a new way to compete. Similarly, the authors cite Compaq as a value innovator in the server business. In the 1990s Compaq created a series of new value curves to stay on top of the server industry. As competitors imitated and converged on Compaq, the company introduced new value innovations to keep the lead. The innovations were in all three platforms—product, service, and delivery. The company sustained its leadership in the server industry through changing its value curves. Despite the competition, Compaq's repeated value innovations made possible its leadership in the industry. The company repeatedly created new blue oceans.

In their 2015 book, Kim and Mauborgne provide several other examples of companies that broke away from their industries and created new value curves to become industry leaders. Prominent examples include Casella Wines (yellow tail), Southwest Airlines, Cirque du Soleil, NetJets, Curves, NABI, and QB House. Casella Wines, an Australian company, studied the underlying structure of the US wine industry and noted that there was enormous convergence in the value curves among the one thousand six hundred competitors in the industry.[6] The premium wines followed the classic differentiation strategy—high price and high value across all the key competitive factors. They were "different in the same way." The budget wines also had value curves that were similar—low prices and low offerings.

Casella Wines shifted the strategy curves by focusing not on competitors but on alternatives and noncustomers. It pursued both value and low cost. It redefined competition in the industry by looking at the demand side. It created a blue ocean. It's wine—"yellow tail"—broke from the competition. "Instead of offering wine as wine, Casella created a social drink accessible to everyone: beer drinkers, cocktail drinkers, and traditional drinkers of wine"[7] Within two years, yellow tail emerged as the number one imported wine in the US. By looking at the alternatives—beers and ready-to-drink cocktails—and the noncustomers, Casella was able to appeal to the mass of alcohol drinkers. It was successful because it changed the industry conditions for competition.

Southwest Airlines redefined the strategy canvas of the airline industry by offering high speed, frequent and flexible departures with low prices to the mass market. It created a blue ocean by altering the factors of competition in the industry by looking across the alternative car industry. It provided a quantum leap in value for travellers through its low-cost business model (Fig. 6.1).

Similarly, Cirque du Soleil, a Canadian company in circus, redefined the nature of the industry. The company decided to compete by departing from the conventional logic of the circus. It combined circus with theatre, thereby providing a new form of entertainment which attracted new customers who did not previously go to circus. The company created a new value curve in the circus industry.

The other examples quoted by Kim and Mauborgne also share the same strategic profile—their strategies were divergent from their industries. They did not follow the other players in the industry. They created their own unique value curves. NetJets created a blue ocean through the concept of fractional ownership of private jets for corporate travellers who form the mass of customers in the aviation industry. By selling fractions of jets, the company was able to give customers the "convenience of a private jet at the price of first-and business—class air travel."[8] Compared to commercial airlines and corporate private jets, NetJets created a superior value curve for itself.

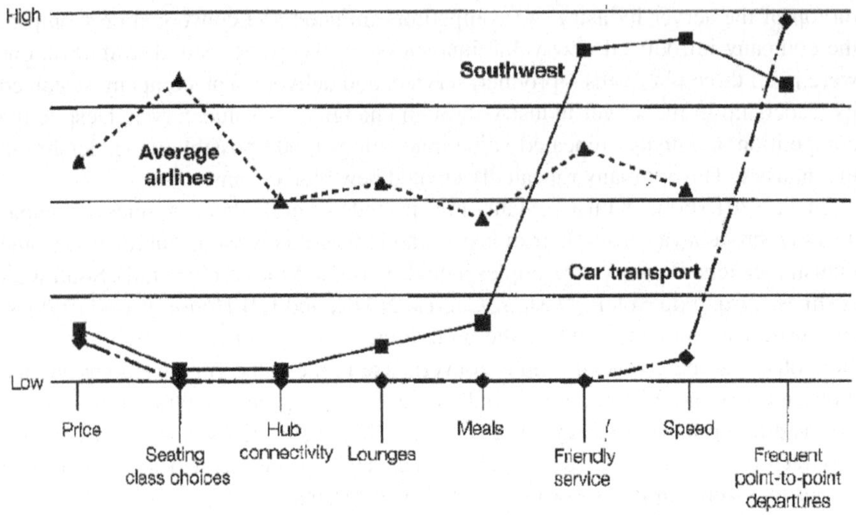

Fig. 6.1 The Strategy Canvas of Southwest Airlines *Source* W. Chan Kim and Renée Mauborgne, Blue Ocean Strategy (Harvard Business Review Press, 2015), p. 41

Curves, NABI, and QB House all created unique differentiations in their respective industries. Curves, a Texas-based woman's fitness company, created demand through its unique value offering to women by looking across strategic groups—combining traditional health club activities and home exercise programmes. By asking what women really wanted, Curves was able to break away from industry trends and success factors and meet the real needs of the mass of women. By focusing on the essentials that the broad mass of women wanted in health and fitness, Curves was able to provide a distinctive value at a low cost. Curves did not compete with other health and fitness providers. It created new demand by combining attractive features of two strategic groups and eliminating everything that was of no value to most women seeking fitness.

NABI, a Hungarian bus company, and QB House, a Japanese beauty business, also broke away from their industries and created blue oceans. NABI adopted fiberglass in making its buses which not only cut cost in preventive maintenance but brought several other benefits to its buyers. It created a value curve that was radically divergent from the industry's average curve. NABI shifted competition from price to values such as corrosion, maintenance cost, fuel consumption, and environmental friendliness. NABI created exceptional value for its buyers.

QB (Quick Beauty) House did the same thing in the beauty business—it created a blue ocean in the Japanese barbershop industry. It did this by shifting the industry from an emotional industry to a functional industry. QB House redefined the haircutting experience for men by reducing the actual time taken for cutting hair. It achieved this by eliminating many activities traditionally provided together with haircutting. It radically changed the industry value curve in terms of cost, waiting time, and hygiene. In other words, QB House performed very differently from the average Japanese barbershop.

Apart from the above cases, Kim and Mauborgne quote many other companies that deployed blue ocean strategy to differentiate themselves from their competitors in the industry. They include Ford, Starbucks, Novo Nordisk, Bloomberg, Cemax, IKEA, Apple, Cisco, Philips, Canon, Dyson, Swatch, Nintendo, and Walmart. All these companies had one thing in common—they did not do what the others in the industry were doing. They did not try to better the competitors. Instead, they created unique value for the customer and for themselves. They reinvented how business was done in the industry. They innovated, profitably.

Two Strategic Logics

Conventional logic (red ocean) and value innovation logic (blue ocean) are based on different thought processes (Table 6.1).

The two strategic logics dictate different strategic thinking, which results in different strategic profiles. To produce different strategies, managers need to think

Table 6.1 Two strategic logics

The five dimensions of strategy	Conventional logic	Value innovation logic
Industry assumptions	Industry's conditions are given	Industry's conditions can be shaped
Strategic focus	A company should build competitive advantages. The aim is to beat the competition	Competition is not the benchmark. A company should pursue a quantum leap in value to dominate the market
Customers	A company should retain and expand its customer base through further segmentation and customization. It should focus on the differences in what customers value	A value innovator targets the mass of buyers and willingly lets some existing customers go. It focus on the key commonalities in what customers value
Assets and capabilities	A company should leverage its existing assets and capabilities	A company must not be constrained by what it already has. It must ask, What should we do if we were starting anew?
Product and service offerings	An industry's traditional boundaries determine the products and services a company offers. The goal is to maximize the value of those offerings	A value innovator thinks in terms of the total solution customers seek, even if that takes the company beyond its industry's traditional offerings

Source W. Chan Kim and Renée Mauborgne, "Value Innovation: The Strategic Logic of High Growth" (Harvard Business Review, January–February 1997), p. 106

differently and make different assumptions about their industries. Same thinking and same industry assumptions will lead to same or similar business strategies. There can be no divergent strategies. The two different strategic logics in Table 6.1 produce two sets of action as shown in Table 6.2—commonly referred to as red ocean strategy and blue ocean strategy.

Table 6.2 explains how red ocean and blue ocean strategies differ in terms of managerial activities. The fundamental tenets of blue ocean strategy are captured in Table 6.2. In blue ocean strategy, companies and managers (1) create uncontested market space, (2) make the competition irrelevant, (3) create and capture new demand, (4) break the value-cost trade-off, and (5) align the whole system of a firm's activities in pursuit of differentiation and low cost. The foundation for the five characteristics of blue ocean strategy is the cornerstone concept of value innovation (Fig. 6.2).

Value innovation is created in the region where a company's actions favorably affect both its cost structure and its value proposition to buyers. Cost savings are made by eliminating and reducing the factors an industry competes on. Buyer value is lifted by raising and creating elements the industry has never offered. Over time,

Table 6.2 Red ocean versus blue ocean strategy

Red ocean strategy	Blue ocean strategy
Compete in existing market space	Create uncontested market space
Beat the competition	Make the competition irrelevant
Exploit existing demand	Create and capture new demand
Make the value—cost trade-off	Break the value-cost trade-off
Align the whole system of a firm's activities with its strategic choice of differentiation or low cost	Align the whole system of a firm's activities in pursuit of differentiation and low cost

Source W. Chan Kim and Renée Mauborgne, Blue Ocean Strategy (Harvard Business Review Press, 2015), p. 18

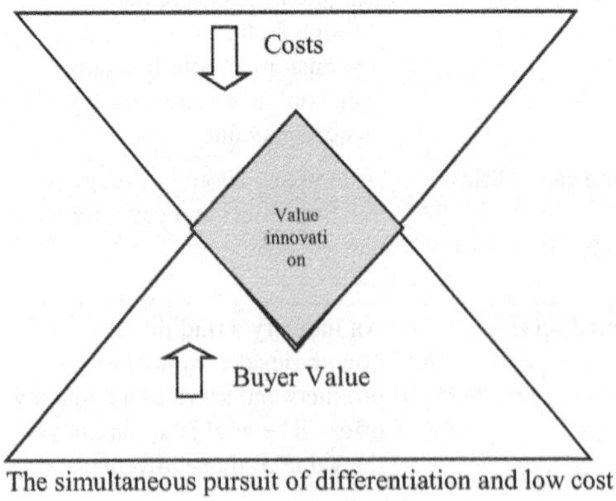

Fig. 6.2 Value innovation: the cornerstone of blue ocean strategy *Source* W. Chan Kim and Renée Mauborgne, Blue Ocean Strategy (Harvard Business Review Press, 2015), p. 17

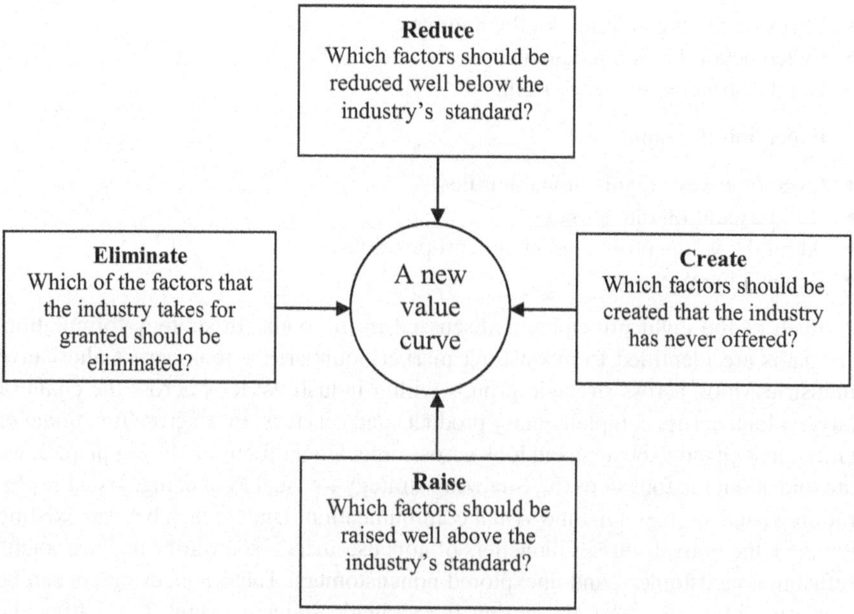

Fig. 6.3 The four actions framework *Source* W. Chan Kim and Renée Mauborgne, Blue Ocean Strategy (Harvard Business Review Press, 2015), p. 31

costs are reduced further as scale economies kick in due to the high sales volumes that superior value generates.

The idea behind blue ocean strategy is simple and straightforward—create value for buyers and the company. Value innovation is not for customers alone. It is also for the business. Innovations must provide not just value to customers but also revenue and profit to the company. Innovation must be profitable. Blue ocean strategy is a system of activities that both reduces cost and increases value for the customer. Cost savings are made by reducing or eliminating factors that companies presently compete on. Value is added by raising or creating new factors in the offerings to customers. The proponents of blue ocean strategy call this "The Four Actions Framework" (Fig. 6.3). The objective is the simultaneous pursuit of differentiation and cost.

Formulating and Executing Blue Ocean Strategy

Kim and Mauborgne lay down eight principles for formulating and executing blue ocean strategy.[9]

Formulation Principles

- Reconstruct market boundaries.

- Focus on the big picture, not the numbers.
- Reach beyond existing demand.
- Get the strategic sequence right.

Execution Principles

- Overcome key organizational hurdles.
- Build execution into strategy.
- Align the value, profit, and people propositions.
- Renew blue oceans.

Each of the eight principles is discussed in the book. In strategy formulation, six paths are identified to reconstruct market boundaries—look across alternative industries; look across strategic groups within industries; look across the chain of buyers; look across complementary products and services; look across functional or emotional appeal to buyers; and look across time. Under focus on the big picture, we are told about the four steps to visualizing strategy—visual awakening, visual exploration, visual strategy fair, and visual communication. Under reach beyond existing demand, the book discusses three tiers of noncustomers—soon-to-be noncustomers, refusing noncustomers, and unexplored noncustomers. These noncustomers can be converted into customers on getting the strategic sequence right. On getting the strategic sequence right, the authors discuss four steps to develop a commercially viable blue ocean idea—buyer utility, price, cost, and adoption. These sequences represent the four tests of any blue ocean idea.[10]

For blue ocean strategy execution, several prescriptive actions are recommended for each of the four execution principles.[11] Four organizational hurdles to strategy execution are identified—cognitive, motivational, resources, and political. The suggested prescription to overcome these organizational hurdles is "tipping point leadership." It is leadership that "focuses on transforming the extremes: the people, acts, and activities that exercise a disproportionate influence on performance. By transforming the extremes, tipping point leaders are able to change the core fast and at low cost to execute their new strategy."[12]

To build execution into strategy, the concept of "fair process" is introduced. Fair process is defined to include three elements—engagement, explanation, and expectation. They are viewed as key to winning employee support for strategic change. The practice of fair process is said to also apply to winning support of external stakeholders critical to strategy execution. In terms of aligning value, profit, and people propositions, the argument made is that all these three elements must come together in a holistic fashion for strategy implementation. They need to be aligned to achieve the twin objective of differentiation and low cost. People proposition includes both internal and external stakeholders, including supply chain partners. When the three strategy propositions are not in alignment, the strategy cannot be sustained. It will fail. The UK charity, Comic Relief, and Apple's iTunes had alignment between the three propositions and therefore achieved sustainability in performance. On the other hand, Tata Nano in cars and Napster in digital music got into trouble because of failure to achieve alignment, in particular to win support of important external stakeholders.

The last principle of blue ocean strategy is renewal of blue oceans—how to sustain the competitive advantage gained. The authors state: "Understanding the process of renewal is key to ensure that the creation of blue oceans is not a one-off occurrence but is institutionalised as a repeatable process in an organisation."[13] They raise the question: "When should a company reach out to create another blue ocean to renew its business or its portfolio of businesses?"[14] The authors believe prolonged sustainability of blue ocean strategy is possible. They state "companies that create blue oceans usually reap the benefits without credible challenges for ten to 15 years."[15] The reason is that "blue ocean strategy creates considerable economic and cognitive barriers to imitation."[16] Imitation requires changing business models and the whole system of activities currently performed by the imitator. Cognitive barriers can be an equally effective obstacle to imitation. It is not easy for cosmetic brands like Estee Lauder and L'oreal to imitate Body Shop without undermining their own current brand images. It is hard to unseat a blue ocean creator. Microsoft's attempt to unseat Intuit as the industry leader in financial software has not been successful. Blue ocean strategy, by going after the mass market, also creates economies of scale that make imitation difficult. High volume produces cost advantages that place imitators at a cost disadvantage. The economies of scale enjoyed by Walmart in purchasing discourage other companies from imitating Walmart's blue ocean strategy. Table 6.3 lists the barriers to imitating blue ocean strategy.

The authors concede that eventually blue ocean strategies will be imitated. When this happens, companies in blue oceans tend to fall into the trap of red ocean strategy—i.e., competing to defend their positions. Value curves tend to converge

Table 6.3 Imitation barriers to blue ocean strategy

Alignment barrier
• Alignment of the value, profit, and people propositions around both differentiation and low cost builds sustainability and hence a formidable barrier to imitation
Cognitive and organizational barrier
• Value innovation does not make sense to a company's conventional logic
• Imitation often requires significant organizational changes
Brand barrier
• Blue ocean strategy may conflict with other companies' brand image
• Companies that value-innovate earn brand buzz and a loyal customer following that tends to shun imitators
Economic and legal barrier
• Natural monopoly: The market often cannot support a second player
• High volume leads to rapid cost advantage for the value innovator, discouraging followers from entering the market
• Network externalities discourage imitation
• Patents or legal permits block imitation

Source W. Chan Kim and Renée Mauborgne, Blue Ocean Strategy (Harvard Business Review Press, 2015), p. 206

with those of competitors. "To avoid the trap of competing, renewal is needed"[17], say the two authors. Renewal means re-innovating and creating new blue oceans. This applies to both single and multi-business firms. Multi-business companies need to renew their portfolio of businesses in blue oceans. At the individual business level, the company needs to constantly monitor the value curves of its competitors. When the value curves begin to converge, it is time for the company to make another blue ocean strategic move.

At the corporate level, a company with multiple businesses should plan and monitor its portfolio of businesses for renewal. Here the authors introduce the concept of pioneers, migrators, and settlers (PMS). Pioneers represent blue ocean businesses, migrators are value improvements, and settlers are me-too businesses. It is the function of corporate strategy to plot the existing portfolio of businesses on the PMS map to achieve a profitable balance between its pioneers, migrators, and settlers. Diversified companies such as Apple, General Electric, Johnson and Johnson, and Procter and Gamble need to maintain a healthy balance across their pioneers, migrators, and settlers. In other words, balance the profit of today and the growth of tomorrow. When iPod became a migrator, Apple launched its next blue ocean (iPhone). When Macintosh sank into red ocean, Apple created iMac (migrator). All diversified companies operate in both red and blue oceans. They need to learn to swim in both oceans at a given point in time and succeed in both. This means they need to understand and apply both blue ocean strategy and competition-based strategy. Companies in different products and businesses need to create not only blue oceans but also compete in red oceans. Red ocean and blue ocean strategies are complementary, serving different purposes.

Timing is important in creating new blue oceans. It should not be too early or too late. A company should not pursue a new blue ocean when there is still profit to be made in the current business. It should resist the temptation to value-innovate when its current value curve has focus, divergence, and a compelling tagline. "It should swim as far as possible in the blue ocean, making itself a moving target… the aim is to dominate the blue ocean over imitators for as long as possible."[18] Body Shop waited too long before seeking a new blue ocean. When its blue ocean turned red with its competitors' value curves converging with its own, the company did not reach out for a new blue ocean and consequently experienced challenges. Understanding how to manage the dynamics of continuous renewal is the key to sustainability.

Is Blue Ocean Strategy All Fluff?

What is the contribution of blue ocean strategy to strategic thinking and practice? Opinion varies—from it is all fluff to a new paradigm in strategic thinking. The authors claim blue ocean strategy is based on data—a study of 150 strategic moves spanning more than 100 years and covering 30 industries.[19] More importantly, they stress that the unit of analysis in blue ocean strategy is not the company or the competitor but the strategic moves companies make to differentiate themselves from others. This is different from the I/O model of Porter with its focus on industry structure and Barney's emphasis on firm resources. Also, the authors point out that much of the strategy literature is on content and not on how to build strategies. In blue ocean strategy, the authors provide tools, frameworks, and principles to guide managers on how to formulate and execute sustainable strategies, not only in business but also in government and social organisations. Blue ocean strategy is prescriptive—it guides managerial actions. It tells managers how to deal with competition and win. It is a recipe book for managers looking for practical answers on how to develop and implement strategies.

The authors of blue ocean strategy provide quantitative evidence that the strategy works. In a study of business launches of 108 companies, they found that 86% of the launches were not blue ocean (they were line extensions). Only 14% were blue ocean launches. But when they compared the revenue and profit impact of the two categories of launches, they found that the line extension launches accounted for only 62% of total revenues and 39% of total profits. The blue ocean launches generated 38% of total revenues and 61% of total profits. The data showed that blue ocean business launches had a greater impact on company performance (Table 6.4).

The prescriptive nature of blue ocean strategy is both its strength and its weakness. The strength is that it tells managers how to go about formulating and implementing sustainable strategies to compete against rivals. The weakness is that it ignores the reality of strategy formulation and implementation in the context of organisational dynamics and decision making. There is no discussion of Mintzberg's "emergent strategy" or Quinn's "incrementalism" or Simon's "bounded rationality." A rational-comprehensive approach to problem analysis and decision making is adopted. The organisation is seen as a rational entity, which it is not. Organisational politics is mentioned, but its full impact on how decisions are made in organisations is not explored.

The same for external stakeholders. There is no discussion of the vital importance of national institutions for business strategy, especially for companies involved in international business. National cultures and institutions significantly influence what companies can and cannot do. A strategy may work in the US but not work in China or Japan because of differences in national culture, institutions, and ideology. Cross-cultural studies clearly show the limitations of Western theories of management

Table 6.4 The profit and growth consequences of creating blue oceans

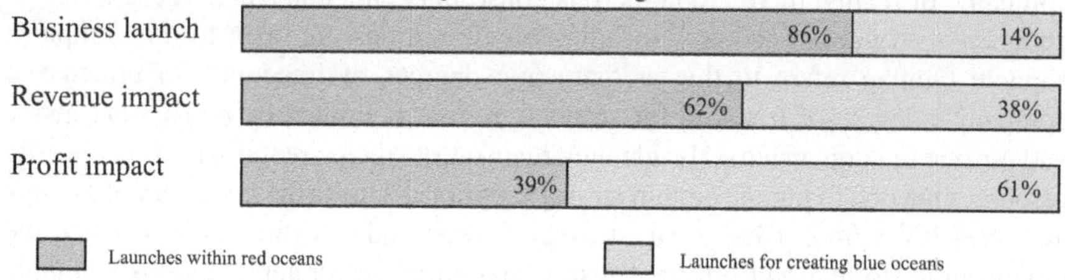

Source W. Chan Kim and Renée Mauborgne, Blue Ocean Strategy (Harvard Business Review Press, 2015), p. 7

when applied to other countries and cultures.[20] Blue ocean strategy has little to say on this. Yet it is presented as a general prescription for strategy formulation and implementation.

There are other challenges that blue ocean strategy has to contend with. Its prescriptive approach to strategy smacks of Taylorism—one best way to manage. People like Mintzberg would argue that there is not even consensus on what strategy is. There are several "schools" of strategy—Mintzberg identifies ten in his book **Strategy Safari**. This means there are different perspectives on strategy and strategy development. Blue ocean strategy is just one perspective. Yet it is presented as the way to strategy formulation and implementation. Much of the push for blue ocean strategy comes from INSEAD, which has made the strategy the foundation for all its management development programmes. Blue Ocean Strategy Institutes in different countries are also active in spreading the blue ocean gospel. There is a need for caution in over marketing blue ocean strategy.

The concern arises because blue ocean strategy is derived from success stories of companies that made certain strategic moves that worked. The authors say they studied 150 strategic moves to come up with the theory of blue ocean strategy. The underlying idea was to look for patterns in the successful strategic moves made by companies. The frameworks, tools, and analyses in blue ocean strategy are derived from this data. One can take issue with this methodology. There is no comparison data for similar strategic moves that failed to produce results for companies. We certainly want to know of companies that made similar strategic moves but failed. This will help us to better understand the causal factors behind blue ocean strategy. There may be other intervening variables behind the success or failure of blue ocean strategic moves. Otherwise, it is difficult to attribute the success of companies to the strategic moves they made. Research by people like Tom Peters and Jim Collins have identified other factors and strategies that account for organisational success.[21] There are companies that attempted to pursue differentiation and low cost (hybrid strategy) and failed. This is a major point made by Porter. These cases are not discussed in the literature on blue ocean strategy. Blue ocean strategy talks about companies that have successfully combined differentiation and low cost. It does not talk about companies that failed to combine differentiation and low cost and got "stuck in the middle" in the process.

Blue ocean strategy assumes a company or organisation is free to choose and act between different courses of action. It assumes there are no limitations on the company. In reality, there are numerous constraints on a company. These limit the company's strategic freedom. Not all strategic options are open to the company. Kenichi Ohmae refers to this as "strategic degrees of freedom." In practice, a company's degree of freedom for strategic moves is limited by constraints inside and outside the organisation. Inside the organisation, there are limitations of specific resources needed to pursue certain strategic options. This is the argument of Barney and the RBV school. Blue ocean strategy does not address this issue. Outside the organisation, formal and informal institutions limit the strategic options available to a company. Blue ocean strategy recognises external stakeholders, but there is no specific analysis or appreciation of the vital role of institutions on the strategic choice a company can make. Peng views institutions as the "third leg" of strategy. No similar treatment is found in blue ocean strategy.

Blue ocean strategy is essentially "inside" oriented—its emphasis is on managerial actions and choices. Its approach to strategy is what Cynthia Montgomery calls the "myth of the super-manager"—a belief that a "competent manager can produce success in virtually any situation."[22] She points out in her book **The Strategist** that there are many competitive forces in the environment that are "beyond the control of most individual companies and their managers."[23] This is a reality that blue ocean strategy does not adequately address. The influence of institutions and the competitive forces of industry are either dismissed in a cavalier fashion or not treated at all in the belief that these forces can be overcome by right strategic choices. Montgomery concedes that "Individual firms on occasions have not only achieved great success in industries where most others have failed, they've even changed the basic competitive context of the industries."[24] But she argues that none of these strategies appeared out of the blue. They came from a deep understanding of the industry and forces at work in them. In other words, the environment is relevant. Although Montgomery is talking about industry and industry forces, her argument applies equally to the larger institutional environment in which companies operate. The blue ocean strategist cannot ignore the constraints—both inside and outside the organisation—that limit his strategic choices. Organisations are not always free to pursue blue ocean strategy. It is not a panacea for competition, as made out to be. Many times, organisations just have to compete in the red ocean.

Blue ocean strategy also runs into problem when viewed in the context of organisational networks. Today, organisations are networked—they function in clusters, not as individual entities. Value and supply chains cut across many different companies. No one company controls the entire value chain from supplier to retailer. This means companies in the network collaborate along functional lines to strategies and deliver products and services in a cost-effective manner. Companies don't compete. It is clusters of companies that compete. This is captured in the concept "no business is an island." The significance of networks in business strategy has been demonstrated in Uppsala studies.[25] The studies show that:

> The performance and effectiveness of organizations operating in a network, by whatever criteria these are assessed, become dependent not only on how well the organization itself performs in interaction with its direct counterparts, but also on how these counterparts in turn manage their relationships with third parties. An organization's performance is therefore largely dependent on whom it interacts with.[26]

Organisations exist and perform in a context. The performance of an organisation is determined by its context. This makes it difficult to define "where the discretion of an organisation, and thus the organisation itself, ends and another begins."[27]

Clearly blue ocean strategy does not fit into the Uppsala model of organisation. Blue ocean strategy is based on individual organisations or companies making their own strategic choices to differentiate themselves from the competitors. It rests on the assumption that organisations have the freedom to make their own strategic choices. Clearly this assumption is not valid if organisations function in networks where no single business entity can make strategic choices independently of the rest in the network. Given that businesses are increasingly working in networks, the relevance of blue ocean strategy as a generic framework for business competition becomes questionable.

Blue ocean strategy also has to deal with two other organisational characteristics—path dependence and isomorphism. Past decisions made by companies resulting in commitment of resources in certain strategic directions cannot easily be reversed without consequences for the company. History and past strategic moves of companies matter. They limit the degree of strategic freedom available to an organisation. Organisations are path dependent. This explains the tendency for organisations to behave incrementally and not embark on quantum changes.

Isomorphism and legitimacy are added challenges to pursuing blue ocean strategy. Blue ocean strategy calls for quantum changes in the way a company competes. It is revolutionary, not incremental. But quantum changes come with a price. When companies break away too far from industry orthodoxy, they risk losing legitimacy in the marketplace. Legitimacy is important because it represents acceptability to stakeholders. Need for legitimacy forces companies to do similar things as their rivals. Organisational behaviour tends to be isomorphic. How different or how same a firm should be is discussed by David Deephouse in his article "To Be Different, Or To Be The Same? It's A Question (And Theory) Of Strategic Balance."[28] This is a relevant question for blue ocean strategy because the strategy is built around being different. The strategic balance that David Deephouse raises between being different from and same as others is not discussed by Kim and Mauborgne in their book on blue ocean strategy. Any theory on strategy that focuses on differentiation needs to address the conflict between differentiation and conformity.

Finally, is there anything new in blue ocean strategy? Or is it old wine in new bottle? The idea of differentiation as a competitive business weapon is not new. It can be traced to Rosser Reeves and his "unique selling proposition" (USP) or to the marketing guru, Ted Levitt who said in his book **Thinking About Management**: "Differentiation is one of the most important strategic and tactical activities in which companies must constantly engage."[29] Porter too identified differentiation as one of the three generic strategies to compete in the market, except that he did not recommend combining differentiation and low cost. He thinks the two are distinct strategies that are not compatible with each other, whereas blue ocean strategy is about combining differentiation and low cost. Does combining differentiation and low cost make blue ocean strategy new? Not really. This was discussed in 1988 by Charles Hill in his article "Differentiation Versus Low Cost or Differentiation and Low Cost: A Contingency Framework."[30] In the article, Hill discusses the contingencies under which differentiation and low cost are compatible. He states "because there often is no unique low cost position, a firm may have to base its sustainable competitive advantage on the simultaneous and continuous pursuit of both low cost and differentiation."[31] In other words, proponents of blue ocean strategy are not the first to question Porter's assertion that generic strategies are mutually exclusive.

The roots of blue ocean strategy can also be traced to Mintzberg's typology of generic strategies where he discussed six different forms of differentiation, thereby expanding and refining Porter's typology of three generic strategies. Mintzberg's discussion of different types of differentiation provided the conceptual clarity for blue ocean strategy.[32]

Perhaps it is to Gary Hamel and C.K. Prahalad that blue ocean strategy owes the most. Many of the concepts and insights in Kim and Mauborgne's book **Blue Ocean Strategy** can be traced to Hamel and Prahalad's book **Competing For The Future**.

Some key insights related to blue ocean strategy found in **Competing For The Future** include:

- Reinventing industry
- Different not better
- Rethinking boundaries of industry
- Changing the rules of competition
- Creating new industries
- Industry transformation
- Inventing the future
- New competitive space
- Identifying discontinuities
- Conceiving new types of customer benefits or conceiving new ways of delivering existing customer benefits
- Strategy is as much about competing for tomorrow's industry structure as it is about competing within today's industry structure
- The need to escape the myopia of the currently served markets should not be a license to ill-conceived diversification
- Radically shifting the basis for competitive advantage in the industry
- Construct unique and non-imitable competitive advantage
- Current and future customers
- Leveraging resources
- Need for foresight
- Radically transforming industry
- Innovation and imagination
- Future is not extrapolation of the past
- White space.

The concept of "white space" in **Competing For The Future** is particularly interesting because it is almost identical to Kim and Mauborgne's "uncontested market space." White space is defined as opportunity to extend existing core competencies into new product markets. Hamel and Prahalad identified Sony, Canon, Sharp and Kodak as companies that took advantage of white space opportunities.

Perhaps an even closer parallel is Gary Hamel's 1996 HBR article "Strategy as Revolution."[33] Many of the insights in this article have found their way into blue ocean strategy in different forms. In the article, Hamel talks about three kinds of companies—rule takers, rule makers, and rule breakers. Blue ocean companies are the rule breakers—the revolutionaries who are against industry orthodoxy. Blue ocean strategic moves are revolutionary in that they redefine industry boundaries and operations. In this context, they fall within Hamel's strategic thinking. Hamel provides the conceptual foundation for much of the theory of blue ocean strategy. In the article, Hamel provides ten principles to guide thinking about strategy creation and nine routes to industry revolution. These principles and routes to strategy creation provide the building blocks for blue ocean strategy.

Is blue ocean strategy, then, all fluff and nothing new? Not quite. While not new in perspective, its contribution lies in taking strategic thinking away from content to process. Its prescriptive approach is valuable. The frameworks and analytical tools provided are of value to managers involved in strategic thinking and strategy creation—especially for those caught in the red ocean. Managers want to know how to create strategies that will work. The structuralists (Porter) provide one model for managerial action and choice. The RBV suggests a different set of analyses and options for the corporate manager. The blue ocean strategy proponents provide yet another course of action for policy makers—the reconstructionist path. Blue ocean strategy is fine, provided it is not peddled as the solution to business strategy making. Strategy making remains an elephantine problem.

Concluding Thoughts

So, where does all this leave us? Are we any closer to knowing what strategy really is, how it is formulated, or how it is implemented? Obviously, we know a lot more today about strategy than the 1960s when the concept first emerged. But that does not mean businesses know how to manage strategy. There is still more confusion than consensus, both in the theory and practice of strategy.

There is no prescription for the strategic manager. There can be no prescription because there is no one best strategy or one best way to formulate strategy. Strategy is contextual. It is developed in response to specific challenges in the business environment and in the context of constraints within the organisation. Both challenges and constraints vary with organisations. Any theory of strategy not built around context is of little help to the strategic manager. Strategy is a course of action chosen to solve specific problems facing an organisation, either now or in the future. In this sense, all strategy is context-bound. Different situations (contexts) call for different strategies. Both the content and process of strategy are not context independent. General theories of strategy can only provide the backdrop for specific context-based strategies. The theories of strategy discussed in this book need to be understood in this light. Despite any claim to the contrary, none of the theories discussed can be a strategy for any specific organisation at any specific time.

In addition, there is the problem of perception. If the purpose of strategy is to solve present or future organisational problems, the way the strategist perceives the problem is crucially important. Problems are perceived not on analysis alone. Given the same analysis, two decision makers can have two different understandings of the problem and therefore two different courses of action (strategy). No amount of analysis will make a difference. Perception is conditioned by many factors, including the personality, fears, and ambitions of the strategic manager. The strategist acts on the basis of his perception of the problem, not on reality. Reality is not knowable. In this context, the emphasis of strategy theories on more and better analysis for strategy making may be misplaced. If strategy is perception, no amount of additional analysis can improve the strategic decision. Strategy theories are too obsessed with analysis to appreciate that reality is perceptual, especially in the context of organisations. A more phenomenological approach will contribute to a better understanding of strategy making.

Another problem with strategy theories is that they assume the strategist has full control over strategy making. This is clearly not the case. All organisations function within various legal and operational constraints imposed by the state. The degree of constraint varies with countries. Generally, there is more government intervention in business operations in emerging and transition societies. Government intervention limits the strategic options available to the decision maker. The decision maker does not have a free hand to adopt strategies that he may consider best for his organisation. Every move that he makes must fall within the policies and regulations set by the government.

Most countries in the developing world are micromanaged through controls, regulations, and policies. In this businesses environment, much of the analysis and prescriptions contained in strategy theories are not relevant to the business manager. His success depends largely on his political skills—his ability to deal with key decision makers in the government bureaucracy. This may change, but for now who you know is more important than strategic thinking or strategic analysis. Here, the institutionalists may have got it right in explaining how strategies work in these societies.

Also, strategy theories assume a high degree of stability in the competitive environment where decisions about long-term directions are possible. Despite what Porter says, strategic thinking and analysis are little relevant when the businesses environment is volatile and turbulent. In an uncertain environment, it is difficult to think long term. Plans become obsolete quickly. The situation is too fluid for any long-term strategy formulation. In this environment, decision making is short-term focused because the long-term directions of the business are murky. In this scenario, the prescriptions in strategy theories are of little help to the business manager. Strategy is like the fire brigade. It cannot know when the next fire will happen or where it will happen. The best it can do is to build its capacity to handle the fire when it does happen.

The strategy models discussed in the book are largely prescriptive, despite claims made otherwise. They tell you how to formulate and implement strategies. What is needed are more descriptive studies of strategy, i.e., how business leaders actually formulate strategies. Such studies can significantly contribute to better strategy theories. The business manager needs more 'grounded' strategy theories to guide his decision making.

The focus of descriptive studies should be on the process of decision making—how strategic choices are actually made, the people involved in them, and the rationale for the choices. How company strategies come into being should be the unit of analysis. What really happens in strategy formulation is key to good strategy theory. To be useful to business decision makers, strategy models must bridge the gap between practice and theory.

To ask which strategy model is the best is meaningless. The various strategy theories and their concepts should be seen as analytical tools to help the business manager better understand his decision environment and consequently make better choices. That is all he should expect from strategy theories. Strategy theories cannot tell him the best strategy for his company.

The global business environment is becoming more volatile and turbulent because of socio-economic and geopolitical changes and disruptive innovations. Volatility and turbulence are becoming the norm. In this business environment, strategy theories based on stability can provide little direction to organisations. To settle on a firm, long-term strategy can be risky. The "best" strategy for business in this environment may well be to make a lot of moves and keep what works. The strategy is similar to that of the entrepreneur. Decisions are more reactive than proactive. You learn as you go along. There is no grand, systemic design that can solve problems for the business manager. Remaining paranoid and entrepreneurial may be the only strategy open to him. This does not mean strategy theories have no value. They have, provided we understand their limitations. In this context, middle-range theories of strategy conceptualized along the lines of Robert Merton may prove to be more relevant to the strategist in business.

No one could have predicted Covid-19 or its ramifications. Businesses have been wiped out despite having successful strategies that had worked for years. It is not enough to have strategies that work. The organisation must develop a strategic mind to continually deal with new challenges and uncertainties. Continuous reinvention is the only option for business success.

It is people who come up with strategies, not organisations. The productive management of people and talent may well be the ultimate key to good strategy making. Where there is space for good men and women to think and act is where you are likely to find the seeds of strategy.

Notes

1. Chan Kim and Mauborgne [1].
2. Mohamed [2].
3. Chan Kim and Mauborgne [3], p. 12.
4. **Ibid.**, p. 17.
5. Chan Kim and Mauborgne [4], p. 108.
6. Chan Kim and Mauborgne [5], p. 29.
7. **Ibid.**, p. 33.
8. **Ibid.**, p. 53.
9. **Ibid.**, p. 23.
10. For a discussion of the four strategy formulation principles, see **ibid.**, Chapters 3, 4, 5, and 6.
11. For a discussion of the four strategy execution principles, see **ibid.**, Chapters 7, 8, 9 and 10.

12. **Ibid.**, p. 168.
13. **Ibid.**, p. 203.
14. **Ibid.**, p. 203.
15. Chan Kim and Mauborgne [6], p. 7.
16. **Ibid.**, p. 7.
17. Chan Kim and Mauborgne [7], p. 207.
18. **Ibid.**, p. 207.
19. **Ibid.**, inside cover page.
20. For a discussion of the impact of culture on management, see Lourdesamy [8], pp. 63–86 and pp. 103–110.
21. See Peters and Waterman [9] and Collins and Porras [10].
22. Cynthia Montgomery [11], p. 23.
23. **Ibid.**, p. 27.
24. **Ibid.**, p. 31.
25. The Uppsala studies (originating at the University of Uppsala, Sweden) adopt a network model to the study of business organisations.
26. Hakansson and Snehota [12], p. 261.
27. **Ibid.**, p. 263.
28. Deephouse [13].
29. Quoted in Trout [14], p. 25
30. Hill [15].
31. **Ibid.**, p. 411.
32. See Mintzberg [16], pp. 83–92.
33. Hamel [17].

References

1. Chan Kim W, Mauborgne R (1997) Value innovation: the strategic logic of high growth. Harvard Business Review
2. Mohamed (Ed.) (2012) Blue ocean strategy insights and experiences of Universiti Sains Malaysia. Penerbit Universiti Sains Malaysia
3. Chan Kim W, Mauborgne R (2015) Blue ocean strategy. Harvard Business Review Press, p 12
4. Chan Kim W, Mauborgne R (1997) Value innovation: the strategic logic of high growth. Harvard Business Review, p 108
5. Chan Kim W, Mauborgne R (2015) Blue ocean strategy. Harvard Business Review Press, p 29
6. Chan Kim W, Mauborgne R (2004) Blue ocean strategy. Harvard Business Review, p 7
7. Chan Kim W, Mauborgne R (2015) Blue ocean strategy. Harvard Business Review Press, p 207
8. Lourdesamy I (2017) New frontiers of management. Cengage Learning Asia, pp 63–86 and pp 103–110
9. Peters T, Waterman R (1982) In search of excellence. Harper and ROW
10. Collins J, Porras J (1994) Built to last. Harper Business Essentials
11. Cynthia Montgomery (2012) The strategist. (Harper Collins, p 23
12. Hakansson H, Snehota I (2006) No business is an island: the network concept of business strategy. Scand J Manage 22:261

13. Deephouse D (1999) To be different, or to be the same? It's a question (and theory) of strategic balance. Strategic Manage J 20
14. Trout J (2000) Differentiate or die. Wiley, p 25
15. Hill C (1988) Differentiation versus low cost or differentiation and low cost: a contingency framework. Acad Manage Rev 13(3)
16. Mintzberg H (1996) Generic business strategies. In: Mintzberg H, Quinn J (eds) The strategy process, 3rd edn. Prentice Hall, pp 83–92
17. Hamel G (1996) Strategy as revolution. Harvard Business Review

Company Index

© The Editor(s) (if applicable) and The Author(s), under exclusive license to Springer Nature Singapore Pte Ltd. 2021
L. Iruthayasamy, *Understanding Business Strategy*,
https://doi.org/10.1007/978-981-33-6542-1

Name Index

© The Editor(s) (if applicable) and The Author(s), under exclusive license to Springer Nature Singapore Pte Ltd. 2021
L. Iruthayasamy, *Understanding Business Strategy*,
https://doi.org/10.1007/978-981-33-6542-1

Subject Index

© The Editor(s) (if applicable) and The Author(s), under exclusive license to Springer Nature Singapore Pte Ltd. 2021
L. Iruthayasamy, *Understanding Business Strategy*,
https://doi.org/10.1007/978-981-33-6542-1

The authorized representative in the EU for product safety and compliance is Springer Nature Customer Service Center GmbH, Europaplatz 3, 69115 Heidelberg, Germany. If you have any concerns about our products, you can contact us on ProductSafety@springernature.com

Printed and bound by CPI Group (UK) Ltd, Croydon, CR0 4YY

The manufacturer's authorised representative in the EU is Springer Nature Customer Service Centre GmbH, Europaplatz 3, 69115 Heidelberg, Germany. If you have any concerns regarding our products, please contact ProductSafety@springernature.com

Printed and bound by CPI Group (UK) Ltd, Croydon, CR0 4YY
30/09/2026
02225306-0006